# *The Magic of*
# Goal Setting

## by John Church

a Network Marketing Support book

Printing History
*First Edition    January 2001*
*Second Edition    December 2002*

A catalogue record for this book is available from the British
Library.

Published by
Network Marketing Support
Heathcote House
1 Heathcote Road
Bordon
Hants GU35 0BN

Tel: 01420 473383
Fax: 01420 476140
Email: orders@aireau.co.uk
Website: www.aireau.co.uk

ISBN: 0 9544342 0 X

Printed in England by Halstan & Co Ltd
2-10 Plantation Road, Amersham, Buckinghamshire HP6 6HJ

*To my wife Anne, who after 30 years continues*
*to teach, train and motivate me on a daily basis!*
*I love you.*

*Also to my two special grown up kids,*
*Karen and Jonathan, who, when children,*
*taught me the power of persistence.*

## What people have said about John's book

Your book took me through a roller coaster ride of emotions – ranging from tears of sorrow to tears of joy. I have learned that I would rather spend one day with a dream than a life time without one.
*Brian James – Amway*

Thank you for writing the "Magic of Goal Setting" I can't wait to share your ideas with some of my team tomorrow night.
*Birgitta Stevenson – Forever Living Products*

I received your book through our business training system and it was wonderful! I've heard you speak so I knew the book would be good. I was so excited I was up half the night reading it. Your book has helped me build my confidence. Thank you very much.
*Ken Moore - NFLI*

Your book is wonderful! The army and squirrel stories amused me and the principles you taught were very thought provoking. I enjoyed it so much. Thank you.
*Ann Riley*

I have just finished reading your book, "The Magic of Goal Setting". I have to say that it has helped me tremendously. It has allowed me to see many of the opportunities I have been missing in life and why I have been unable to see them. I just wanted to let you know that your book has touched a life all the way from Houston, Texas.
*Roy Francione – Legacy for Life*

I think your book is excellent. I found it easy to read and inspirational. As a result, some new people have been sponsored and I am keen to do much more. Thanks for making such a valuable contribution to my training and motivational level. Please write more books!
*Jenny Rich – Amway*

I have spent thirty years teaching motivation and personal development to people from all walks of life, and presenting Goal Setting in an easy to understand way is a rare talent. This book is a must read for anyone you know who struggles with keeping to commitments and therefore fails to determine their own future. This book makes it simple for anyone to decide their own destiny.
*Larry Brooks – Neways International (UK)*

I have just finished reading your book "The Magic of Goal Setting". I thought it was absolutely fantastic!!!!!! It was the most simplified and direct book I have read on the subject of goals. You broke it down so that it can be accomplished with minimal effort and also fun to do. The humour only made it so much more fun to read. My life will not be the same again.
*Jeanne Sabate – NFLI*

I have read your book " The Magic of Goal Setting" several times now. WOW! I have taken many courses and read many books on goal setting but yours has really hit home for me and explained the philosophy behind this diverse subject!
*Nancy Lacasse – Quality Life Improvement Specialist*

Congratulations!–I've just spent two hours lying in the bath reading "The Magic of Goal Setting" from cover to cover. It is excellent and we will certainly be recommending that all our Distributors purchase a copy.
*Tony and Vhonda Morcom – NFLI*

# About the Author

The Magic of Goal Setting is John's first book which has proved to be a phenomenal success both in the USA and the UK. Due to the demand, this second enlarged edition has been released. The 'message' remains unchanged, this coupled with John's enthusiastic and humorous approach to the subject, ensures that "The Magic of Goal Setting" is destined to become a classic.

John has been involved in the network marketing sector for over 20 years. Within that period he has owned and sold his own party plan company as well as achieving the 'top distributor' position in two separate companies. This experience of having worked both sides of the fence, has given John a unique understanding of the industry that few others can match.

His success in network marketing has enabled John to achieve financial security, allowing him to indulge in his passion for travel, sport and public speaking. He currently spends time between his homes in England, Ireland and South Africa.

John has become known internationally for his dynamic and unique style as a Network Marketing trainer and motivational speaker. He teaches in pictures and stories, often humorous, which participants can relate to and, more importantly, remember.

John specialises in networking, leadership, health and goal setting keynote presentations. He has inspired thousands of people across Europe, South Africa and America with his motivational seminars and continues to help people gain control of their lives through positive action. He is well known in the industry and his personal success has been recorded in several international magazines.

Philip Rudland – Network Marketing Support

**TRAINING AND SEMINARS** (see page 123)

# Contents

# From Failure to Success

Twenty years ago, long before I owned my own network marketing company and before I was even successful as a network marketing distributor, I was a complete flop.

At the tender age of 15, I got expelled from school. Nothing too drastic—I just enjoyed other activities more than turning up for school everyday! Unfortunately, the authorities had noted my poor attendance and had unexpectedly turned up at my home one evening. I had just returned from a day out in London and was still wearing my school uniform.

I answered the door to a bespectacled man complete with cycle clips and a heavy duty green Raleigh bicycle.

"Are your parents at home?" he enquired.

You don't have to be a rocket scientist to realize your immediate future is in serious danger. My parents were definitely not impressed. At the end of term I was asked to leave. No education certificates, no prospects, no discipline, and no money—so I joined the Army!

Somehow the powers that be decided that I had certain qualities. They believed that with the right training I could be a Land Surveyor. They were right—it's just that their timing was wrong. For the first seven years I failed just about every exam. Finally I had my confidential report read to me. It stated, "This man has reached his ceiling." I was 24 years old.

Sometimes in life you just get lucky.

My luck came in the form of a pretty young girl called Anne. For the first time in my life someone believed in me. Even my mother tried to persuade Anne that she should look elsewhere!

"He never concentrates on anything and if you married him it wouldn't last five minutes," my Mum told her none too subtly. I was standing next to Anne at the time!

We married in 1970 and as I write this book we have just celebrated thirty years of marriage.

My Army career started to move thanks to Anne's gentle support, encouragement and understanding. For the first time in my life I started to focus. Slowly I started to believe that I could become a competent surveyor. At last I started to pass exams, which resulted in promotions.

Now that my Army career was back on track and I was making steady progress my thoughts turned to money – or rather the lack of it. By now we had two beautiful children and money was tight. Every month seemed to have more days in it than my salary could cover. What could I do to generate some extra income? A friend introduced me to network marketing. I was skeptical—it sounded like "selling."

I went to business opportunity meetings and sat in the back row. I listened to speakers talk about wealth, prosperity, and freedom, and concluded, "He's not talking to me. There's no way I could ever be in that position."

But for some reason I still don't quite understand, I got into network marketing anyway! I suppose that while I never believed I could be as successful as these speakers, I did know that I needed to make some changes in my life. I was broke. So I joined.

My sponsor probably doubted my commitment, but he kept after me to learn about how to change. I can remember my sponsor saying, "John, you need to be at this seminar. There's a guy called Jim Hoyt who is coming over to do a goal-setting seminar. Be there—whatever it takes!"

I didn't want to go.

The cost of the seminar, the hotel room, the food, and the trip to London were more than I could afford. But he kept after me, and I decided to go. I actually went and borrowed the money, and hoped it would change my life.

It did!

In fact, this was probably the best two days I've ever spent in my life, and certainly the best money I'd ever spent. After that day, my life did change—dramatically. I went from being a failure to a success. After that seminar, success became habitual for me. Success was no longer something that only other people had.

Now, my network marketing business took off along with my Army career.

'No's' became 'yes's,' 'suspects' became 'prospects,' and 'I can't do it,' became 'I *can* do it.'

As if by magic my whole life changed for the better and that magic is within everyone (yes, even you!) just waiting to be unleashed.

I suspect you are already in some kind of network marketing business, but if not, I would strongly recommend you investigate the potential of this awesome business.

Last year network marketing did over £50 billion pounds worldwide, and many marketing experts believe that this form of marketing is the way of the future. The simple reason for this is that most people do network marketing every day, they just don't get paid for it. I think if you're already doing the work, you might as well get paid for it.

Let me explain.

True network marketing is just about recommending or promoting—not selling.

Let me explain what I mean. Let's say that you look in your local paper and see that the film *Jurassic Park* is being shown at your local cinema. That night, you go and see it with your wife and two children. You buy four tickets, four Cokes, four bags of popcorn and you watch the film – and it's a great film—

the dinosaurs don't look like Godzilla, they look real. The whole cinema shakes with the terrific Dolby Surround Sound system—and the lawyer gets eaten by the dinosaur! Everybody really enjoys the movie.

Next day at work, as you are standing by the coffee machine, along comes your best friend Ted. Now, do you tell Ted about the exciting time you had raking up leaves in your back garden or do you tell him about the great movie that you saw last night?

"Hey Ted," you say. "You should take your family to see *Jurassic Park*. It's a great movie, and your family will love it."

That night Ted takes his family to see *Jurassic Park*. They buy four tickets, four Cokes, four bags of popcorn and they all think it's a great movie, too. The dinosaurs look real, the seats are shaking with the great Dolby Surround Sound system and the lawyer gets eaten again. That weekend Ted visits his relatives and recommends that they go and see *Jurassic Park* and in turn his relatives recommend and promote the film to all their friends. By the end of the month, hundreds of people have been to see *Jurassic Park* at the local cinema all because you recommended and promoted the film to Ted who in turn recommended and promoted the film to his relatives and friends.

The cinema owner says, "Hey, we did really good this month: hundreds of people came to see *Jurassic Park*. I know we advertised in the local paper, but not many people came because of this; most people came because of the word-of-mouth advertising that was started by you. Therefore I would like to send you a cheque for 10% of the profits as a reward for verbally recommending and promoting the film to your friends and relatives."

Does this happen? No, of course not. The cinema owner

pockets all the profits, but you did network marketing. You just didn't get paid.

True network marketing is not about selling; in fact, only 5% of people even like sales. The other 95% *hate* sales, but most people like to promote and recommend products and services which they think are good value for money.

Here's another example of network marketing.

Let's say you notice a new restaurant called Chez Nous opening in your area. That night you decide to check it out. You arrive and are immediately impressed by the Maitre d' who organizes someone to take your coat and shows you to your table. All the waiters are smartly dressed and have white cloths over their arms. There's a string quartet playing beautiful music in the corner and your table has a wonderful flower arrangement. Your starters and main course are beautifully presented with wonderful flavours, and the sweet trolley is out of this world. Over coffee and mints the bill is discreetly placed next to you and when you pick it up, you're amazed at the low cost of the meal—it really is great value for money.

Next day at work, as you are standing by the coffee machine, along comes your good friend Bill. Now do you tell Bill about the exciting time you had washing your car or do you tell him about the great restaurant that you visited last night?

"Hey, Bill," you say. "You should take your family to Chez Nous. It's a great restaurant and your family will love it."

That night Bill takes his family to Chez Nous and they all think it's a great restaurant, too. That weekend, Bill visits his relatives and recommends that they go and eat out at Chez Nous and in turn his relatives recommend and promote the restaurant to all their friends. By the end of the month, hundreds of people have been to the restaurant all because you recommended and promoted the restaurant to Bill who in turn recommended and promoted it to his relatives and friends.

The restaurant owner says, "Hey, we did really good this month. Hundreds of people came to eat at Chez Nous and most of them came because of the word-of-mouth advertising that was started by you. Therefore I would like to send you a cheque for 10% of the profits as a reward for verbally recommending and promoting my restaurant to your friends and relatives."

Does this happen? No, of course not. The owner pockets all the profits, but you did network marketing. You just didn't get paid.

Network marketing companies simply pay you a word-of-mouth bonus cheque for recommending and promoting their products or services.

Now here's an interesting question.

"If most people do network marketing every day, why don't more people join a network marketing company and collect a cheque every month?"

Answer in a nutshell—ignorance! They don't *know* they can—or they don't *think* they can!

> Jesus walked into a restaurant somewhere in the Western World. He approached three sad-faced gentlemen at a table, and greeted the first one:
> "What's troubling you, brother?" he asked.
> "My eyes. I keep getting stronger and stronger glasses, and I still can't see."
> Jesus touched the man, who ran outside to tell the world about his now 20-20 vision.
> The next gentleman couldn't hear Jesus' question, so The Lord just touched his ears, restoring his hearing to perfection. This man too ran out the door, probably on his way to the audiologist to get a hearing-aid refund.

The third man leapt from his chair and backed up against the wall, even before Jesus could greet him. "Don't you come near me, man! Don't touch me," he screamed, "I'm on disability!"

Some people will see network marketing as a chance to get "healed" and some others will stand up and shout, "Don't get near me, I'm on disability!" If we listen to the disability thinkers long enough, we'll start thinking they're right, because most of us have a well-developed sense of inferiority by the time we reach our early teens. Society moulds us to be average, to fit into the normal run of things, to be part of the crowd.

This is the world we live in. These are the people we share it with. Even if we do give them the secret to changing their lives, they won't take the secret and use it. They'll simply say, "Oh sure, that would work—but not for *me*."

The fact that you are reading this book should tell you something about yourself. God designed you to reach and stretch and to achieve great things. This book is written for you. I want to show you how to take the ceiling off your potential so you can grow at will and succeed in the theatre of life.

# How I Was Introduced To Goals — Other People's Goals

At age 17, I enlisted in the British Army. For the next 25 years, I bravely protected England from a surveyors shortage. Yes, I observed, measured and charted land, producing semi-accurate maps. Now, some people might not consider that an exciting, danger-filled career. These people might even consider surveying a boring occupation. But not the Army. They had goals. They wanted to make our work meaningful and exciting. How? They would send us to exotic locations, where no man had gone before. And leave us there.

Let me give you an example. One year the Army flew me and my surveying partner to the inhospitable, barren, north Arctic region. Yes, I was an Arctic explorer. This was the Army's goal, not mine. I quickly learned that achieving other people's goals wasn't much fun.

In the Arctic, the weather is bad. It's either extremely cold, extremely freezing, or really awful. Since this Arctic exploration was the Army's goal, not mine, I earned roughly the same pay as if I was stationed in the Caribbean. Trust me. I'd rather have been earning my Army pay in the Caribbean.

The Army's goal was for my partner and I to map the uninhabited, desolate, freezing islands of the Arctic. My partner and I had a different goal, and that was to come back alive. This is how we learned the importance of totally focusing on your goal. Because if you weren't totally focused on your personal survival, you wouldn't survive in those conditions. There was no one else around for hundreds of miles to help you. In other words, you were on your own.

Excuses didn't count. Why? Because there was no one within 500 miles to listen to them. If the wind was high and your tent blew away, you froze to death. You could curse the wind, say to the wind, "It's your fault, you blew too hard," but in the end, no matter what your excuse, you froze to death.

The Army would fly us to a spot in the middle of nowhere. We had to be flown there because no boat could get through the ice. We were hundreds of miles from a dentist, an outpost, or civilisation. Three or four days later, they would attempt to come back and collect us.

The pilots hoped they would remember where they dropped us off. It was easy to drop us off—the real challenge was to find that spot again. Compasses don't work very well near the North Pole. Maps? Well, we were there *creating* those maps, so the present maps in the pilots' possession were definitely suspect. A quarter of an inch on their maps could represent 20 miles in the middle of nowhere. There weren't any street signs, roads or motorways.

And if that wasn't bad enough, our little three- and four-day camping trips were in polar bear territory. The pilots jokingly referred to us as "polar bear bait." This wasn't exactly true. The polar bears looked at us as a main meal. We always slept with one eye open. We listened for any sounds that might mean approaching polar bears. And we never cooked. Cooking a meal would just be an advertisement for a polar bear buffet. Focus? Yes! We didn't want to be lunch.

The Arctic taught me the importance of having a focused goal, and how to use activities to achieve that goal, which generally meant coming back alive. The Army did me a favour. They thought they were sending me to the frozen nowhere to make a map. In reality, they were teaching me a lifelong system for achieving goals.

The British Army is very generous. No, they didn't pay us a

lot, but they did invest a lot of time in teaching me how to focus on the goal of staying alive.

Next, they sent me to Kenya. (Again, this was the British Army's goal, not mine.)

At least Kenya wasn't cold. The Army didn't need maps of the inhabited areas of Kenya. They already had those maps. They needed maps of the most desolate, uninhabited, lion- infested areas of the country. This was a job for us, the surveyors' Ninja SWAT team.

Our unarmed team of brave surveyors no longer had to worry about polar bears. Now we had to worry about lions.

Our goal was not to become lion food. Our thoughts were, "The lions are fast and strong. Let them catch some fast, dangerous game and leave us slow, unarmed surveyors alone. Not much sport in catching and eating us."

So, every night we slept with one eye open and listened for any sign of lions. Fortunately for us, the Kenyan government supplied our surveying team with two local Kenyans with guns. This made us feel a bit safer, but we knew our survival was ultimately up to us. We couldn't make excuses such as, "The lion ate me when the Kenyan soldier wasn't looking." Excuses don't count when dealing with lions.

Did we ever come across lions? Yes, sort of. I never actually *saw* the lions, but I knew they were out there comparing us with their other menu options.

For instance, one day I went jogging. Just me, some running shoes and some running shorts. That's it. While I was running, I noticed a large lion's paw print in the ground ahead of me. That immediately brought my original goal of survival back in focus. My heartbeat was probably 150 beats a minute from jogging, but it immediately increased to 250 beats.

I thought, if I was to see the lion right now, what would I do? Run? I was already running. I knew I couldn't outrun a lion. I also knew I couldn't negotiate an acceptable agreement with a lion.

By re-focusing on my goal, which was survival, I instantly made a U-turn and sprinted to camp. This ended my African bush jogging career. I knew that the activity of jogging wasn't going to help me reach my goals. I learned that if your present activity isn't getting you closer to your personal goals, then change the activity. More about this important point later.

On another night, while sleeping in the tent, we heard a cough. The Kenyans and surveyors looked at each other and nodded in agreement that the cough came from outside. Now the Kenyans were more experienced at the focused goal of survival. Before we surveyors had a thought of what to do next, the Kenyans leaped out of the tent, jumped into the cab of the three-ton Army truck, rolled up the windows and locked the doors. The Kenyans had graciously showed us that immediate action helps you achieve your goals.

The surveyors sat in the tent, stunned. We were sure we'd be an entrée at any moment. We waited some more, barely daring to breathe. Finally, our nerves got to us. We ran from the tent to the truck and motioned for the Kenyans to let us in the cab with them. The Kenyans wouldn't open the door. I guess they wanted to reinforce in the surveyors the importance of immediate action.

Well, we got the message that immediate action was best. We jumped into the back of the truck and hoped the lions wouldn't be inclined to jump in the back of the truck with us. We were still exposed to the lions if they were hungry enough, but we couldn't think of anywhere else to go. After about twenty minutes of no lion sightings, the Kenyans opened the doors of the truck cab and announced that the crisis was probably over. We graciously thanked the Kenyans for so brilliantly reinforcing the fact that immediate action was good for survival. We also made a mental note that next time we surveyors would be the first to run for the truck cab and the Kenyans could stay in the back of the truck as potential lion appetisers.

My Army career taught me that immediate, decisive action is always needed to achieve your goals. You can't just loiter around and hope something good happens. Lions and polar bears have a wonderful way of focusing the mind on achieving certain goals.

Achieving less dramatic goals takes the same determination, you just end up wishing some people could get chased by a polar bear just once so they wouldn't complain quite so loudly.

Lets focus in on a few days in the life of my friend Brian.

# The Life of Brian

"Aaaacckkk! A £15 bank charge? Our chequebook account is overdrawn again! Why can't the bank just put a little *extra* money in my account every month?"

Brian was upset, and this lousy day was getting worse. How did the day start? Let's see how the world decided to dump on Brian.

Brian starts his day by cursing his 16-year old car. "Why can't you start, you bucket of bolts and rust? I'm already late for work!"

After his neighbour jump-starts his car for the third time this month, Brian fights his way through rush hour traffic, hoping to make up the thirty minutes he's lost already.

Brian curses, "If it wasn't for all these other people on the road, I wouldn't be late for work. It's not my fault that everyone in town decided to be on the road this morning. You can't blame me for being late. It's those other cars' fault."

Brian arrives at work and notices that he left the Wilson report at home. "Oh no! We have the big Wilson meeting in fifteen minutes and I forgot the report. It's not my fault. The stupid alarm clock went off twenty-five minutes late and I had to clean up the dog's mess. I told my kids not to get a dog. Those useless animals! They're nothing more than continuous poo machines."

The Wilson meeting is a disaster. There's no report, and, of course, no progress. It's a complete waste of time for everyone attending.

Brian's boss takes him aside after the meeting and says, "Brian, we need to talk. Your performance is awful. You haven't completed a single project on time and now you're making me look bad."

"Hey, it's not my fault," replies Brian. "Ron in accounting can never get the figures to me in time. And, I asked for a secretary to help produce these reports, but budgeting turned me down. Plus, I had a dentist appointment last week. My teeth have really been bothering me. Nobody else around here cares about my projects. They all seem to be concerned only about their pet activities. And I can't work Saturdays. My car won't stand the extra wear and tear, and I coach the local soccer team. I'm doing my best with this bad situation, so don't blame me. It's not my fault."

"That's what I wanted to talk to you about, Brian," his boss countered. "It's *never* your fault. You're the man of ten thousand excuses, and all of them are pretty sorry. But here is reality. Excuses don't count. If you don't have the Wilson report on my desk by tomorrow morning, we lose the account—and you lose your job. Wilson doesn't care about your dental appointments and neither do I. The report or your job. Got it?"

The rest of Brian's day was even worse.

The Managing Director stopped by Brian's desk that afternoon. "Brian, step outside with me, would you please?" Brian stepped outside into the parking area.

The Managing Director put his arm around him and said, "Do you see that big hill over there? Pretty, isn't it? Well Brian, someday, if you work really, really hard, if you put your whole heart and soul into your work, there will be a brand new mansion on top of that hill. And that big mansion, with the manicured landscape, and the wonderful gardens, all that will be *mine*... if you work hard and do your job. So Brian, why not get a bit more focused and get that Wilson report on your boss' desk by tomorrow morning?"

This really upset Brian. He thought, "I'm working overtime, literally a slave to this Company, and all my work is just so that the Managing Director can achieve his goal of a new mansion?

Why am I condemned to work on achieving *his* goals and dreams? What about me?"

Brian returned to his desk to read the latest Company memo: *All salaries will be reduced 10% effective immediately. Company profits need to be enhanced to fulfil stockholders' expectations. Thank you for your understanding.*

"Understanding? Understanding? I need a raise, not a cut in pay. I'm already two mortgage payments behind!" Brian went home that evening a bit depressed.

After the aggravation of the overdrawn cheque account, Brian grabbed a beer and sat down to watch the news. Murder, fire, war and other depressing events were carefully described in graphic detail. Better grab another beer.

Brian checks the clock and it's already 7:30 p.m.

"Whoa! I have an opportunity meeting to attend this evening. I don't know why I should go. This network marketing business just isn't working out. I can't sponsor anybody. And, it's getting late already. Maybe I will just skip this meeting. I don't have any guests. I do have to work on that Wilson report. My favourite show is coming on television in thirty minutes. It may start to rain. I already know how the meeting ends. I should say 'hello' to my family. My car might not start. It's the same old meeting hype week after week. My leg is falling asleep. I haven't even had a chance to eat dinner yet. The networking business just isn't growing on its own. My sponsor is a jerk. I bet our dog made a mess again. I need another beer."

Brian misses the opportunity meeting, doesn't finish the Wilson report, wonders why nothing ever gets done, and wishes the world would stop dropping bad fortune his way.

On the plus side, Brian does get to watch his favourite television show.

This is the life of Brian. Compare this to a few days in the life of Tricia.

# The Life of Tricia

Tricia wakes up when she is tired of sleeping. It's 8:45 a.m. and it looks like a great morning to have an outdoor breakfast with her networking leaders at the Hilton. Tricia makes her regular morning telephone call to her daughter at University.

"Hey, how are you getting on with those tennis lessons?"

"I hope to get to the tennis lessons soon. With mid-term exams next week and all the social activities, it's a little hard to squeeze everything in. I'll let you know when you phone tomorrow morning." Tricia's daughter enjoys tennis, but also believes in balance in her life. What's a great tennis game without a social life?

Tricia jumps in her new bonus car to go to the Hilton hotel.

"Great morning, isn't it?" Tricia hears as she arrives for breakfast. "Did you know that John promoted two new distributors to Executive last Saturday? That new training on leadership transforms workers into achievers, don't you think?"

Tricia replies, "That's great news to start the morning. How many people here completed your goals from last week?"

Around the table, each leader gives their goal progress report:

"I sponsored two new distributors at Thursday's opportunity meeting."

"My goal was to pass out one introductory audio cassette tape a day. I only completed my goal five out of the seven days."

"I finished my third class in public speaking. Only seven more to go. I think I will eventually stop blushing when I talk."

"Finished my newsletter, as usual. This goal achievement exercise makes things easy."

"Turned another negative distributor into a doer. Got her setting new goals that she can achieve. She's feeling really confident now."

"Tried sponsoring one new person. Didn't achieve my goal, but now I do have three new prospects considering our opportunity."

"Lost three pounds on our new diet product. Soon I'll be a walking advertisement."

What's going on at Tricia's breakfast meeting?

Sure, leaders are supposed to be positive, but isn't this almost too positive to believe?

Why are these leaders so excited?

They have discovered a simple goal achievement technology that has literally changed their lives.

They can move confidently from one goal to another, and know that they'll achieve their goals quickly, easily, and never have to worry about failure.

Sound too good to be true?

Maybe at first glance, but knowledge is power. Once you see how goals work and how to easily achieve them, you'll become a believer, too.

# Are Goals Really Important?

In 1952 the graduating class from Harvard Business School were asked to take part in a survey. It was a wide-ranging survey with many questions, but the researchers were only really interested in the answer to one question. "Do you have written down goals?" Out of all the graduating students only 3% had written down their goals. Twenty years later, in 1972, they went back to these same people and conducted another lengthy survey, and again they were only interested in the answer to one question: "What is your net worth?" The results of the survey showed that the 3% of graduates who had written their goals down back in 1952 were worth more than the combined net worth of the other 97% of graduates.

## REASONS WHY PEOPLE DON'T SET GOALS

So if goals are so important why don't more people set down their goals in writing? Well, let me give you five reasons.

*Number One would be that they just don't understand or believe in the importance of goal-setting.* Suppose I was to tell you that my network marketing company could field a soccer team that would beat our full International side every time. You're probably thinking, "How could this be possible?" Well, of course, the International team would have to be blindfolded. Now I know what you're thinking— that's ridiculous, John—how do you expect them to hit the goal if they can't see it? But the point is, "How do you expect to hit your goals when you don't have any to aim for?"

*Number Two is that they just don't know how—* after all, goal setting is a skill that is not taught in school. In fact, it's not taught in College or University, either. Even your parents probably didn't teach you how to set goals, so how would you know?

*The third reason people don't set goals is that they don't like to be criticised.* How many times have you told your friends that you're going to quit smoking or lose some weight or start an exercise program or go on a low fat diet? The next minute they see you lighting up after a fish and chip supper and don't they just enjoy reminding you of your recent ambitions?

*Number Four is that people have a fear of failure.* They feel comfortable achieving average results, but the late President John F. Kennedy said that life was not meant to be a prison where we just hang around, waiting to die. He went on to say that we were individually designed so that we could reach and stretch and achieve great things with our lives.

And finally, *the fifth reason people don't set goals is that they just don't take the time to do it.* They procrastinate. There's always a reason like "When the children go back to school, I'll have more time," or "When the warmer weather arrives," or "When I get back from holiday," or "As soon as I'm less busy at work." Does this sound familiar? The plain fact is that setting goals dramatically improves your time management. You become super-efficient and achieve far more with your precious time.

## GOALS ARE SIMPLY DREAMS
## WITH A TIME LIMIT ON ACHIEVEMENT!

Let's take a few moments to do a simple exercise to discover where you are right now! In other words, let's take a quick look at your present lifestyle.

To do this, take a piece of paper and draw out a 4" diameter circle. Divide this circle into eight equal segments using four straight lines, which will create eight spokes. Now think about eight areas of your life that are really important to you in defining your ideal lifestyle. I will give you some examples, but its very important you substitute your own if they are important to you. Now I might select Family, Occupation, Social, Financial, Health, Spiritual, Hobbies and my Network Marketing business. Write these subjects around the outside of the circle— one next to each of the spokes. Now assume that the centre of the circle is '0' and the outside is '10.'

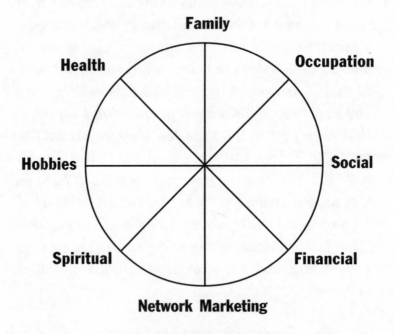

Make a cross on each spoke to indicate how important that quality is to you. For example, if family life were 5 out of 10, you would put a small cross half way along the spoke that had family at the end. Continue to do this for all eight subjects. Then, join the crosses. You will probably find the resulting shape very irregular.

If the front wheel of your bicycle was this shape, you wouldn't get too far, would you? And it's the same in Life. An ideal and happy lifestyle is one where you have *all these important areas of your life in balance*. Ideally, you should be 7 or 8 in all areas of your life that are important to you. If your Social Life is 9 and your Health is 2, you are *not* living your ideal lifestyle!

# Simple Goal-Setting — Incredible Results — Check it Out!

How?

Start small.

Then get bigger.

You don't have to be a goal-achieving rocket scientist to make this plan work. Have you ever seen someone learn something new? They usually start with a simple concept and build new information gradually. Babies learn to take one step first before they learn to walk. Weight lifters start with smaller weights and add more weights as their technique and muscular development increase.

When I decided to start running marathons, I didn't just go out and run 26 miles. Instead, I started running one mile. After my body adjusted to running one mile, I started running two miles at a time, and so on. Finally, after months of daily training, I entered and finished my first marathon.

We're going to do the same thing with our goal muscles and build some confidence. Let's get started with a simple goal exercise that anyone can do.

Breathe.

Yes, breathe. Inhale a breath of fresh air, pause, and exhale.

Not too hard, was it? Do you think you can do it again? I hope so. I bet you've set this little breathing goal millions of times in your life and achieved it every time. You're naturally a goal achievement machine!

Every day you literally set hundreds or even thousands of little goals, and you achieve them. It's so easy that you hardly give it any thought.

Don't let anyone tell you goal setting and goal achieving is difficult. These activities are not difficult and you're *already a professional.*

Want more proof?

How often have you set a goal to go to bed at night?

Have you ever set a goal to wake up in the morning?

Did you set a goal to eat lunch today?

Did you set a goal to watch your favourite television show last night?

Of course you set and achieve these types of goals every day. We take ourselves for granted, as we truly are goal achievement machines.

Did you ever set a goal to get some ice cream? Maybe you checked your home freezer and found it to be ice-cream-free. So, you put on your coat, climbed into your car, fought traffic, braved the rain, drove to the nearest grocery store, and finally purchased some delicious ice cream.

There is no stopping us when we are on a goal achievement journey.

Make your goals immediate.

We are programmed as short-term thinkers. Small, immediate goals are much easier for us to grasp than long-term, lifelong goals. For instance, it's hard for us to visualise making a goal of thirteen million continuous breaths over a period of years. We simply concentrate on meeting the immediate goal of our next breath.

Are long-term goals tough?

No. They just have to be approached as a series of smaller, short-term goals.

If we try making our goals long-term, the goal becomes philosophical, hard to touch and feel, and because its completion is far into the future, procrastination becomes a factor.

Just think of all the New Year's goals that are broken within the first thirty days. Remember that we are programmed to be better short-term thinkers than long-term thinkers.

I told you that in the arctic, we settled for slightly imperfect surveys in exchange for coming back in one piece. Coming back in one piece wasn't something that could be accomplished by "positive thinking." And it wasn't something that could happen even by having the long-range goal of staying alive. It could only occur from achieving hundreds of smaller goals.

---

## Coming back in one piece meant...

Walking at a slow enough pace so that we wouldn't start to sweat and have the sweat freeze causing "frostbite." Too many arctic novices come back with the nickname Three Finger.

Watching every step to avoid a broken leg on the treacherous ice... There were no convenient ambulances!

Warming our rations under our clothing before eating it so that frozen food wouldn't make us nauseous...and as an added bonus we wouldn't alert the polar bears to our whereabouts with a cooking fire.

Never touching a piece of cold metal with our bare hands so they would not instantly freeze in place!

---

The focus was always on that instant: "What will I do right now to stay alive?" In the arctic, each measured step, and every careful move was part of much larger goal—getting home in one piece!

Thankfully, life in business is much easier than staying healthy at the North Pole. But the question is very similar: "What will I do right now to stay in business?"

Not sure what I'm getting at? Here are some more real world examples....

Oh, no! Not cigarettes!

Let's take a long-term goal, and break it down to a workable short-term activity.

Maybe you want to stop smoking. Try setting the goal of never, ever smoking another cigarette as long as you live. Tough, isn't it? This goal is doomed to failure.

However, we can break this goal down into little, bitty parts that are much easier to achieve. Then we can gradually build our long-term goal muscles as our nicotine addiction decreases. Here's how:

Set a goal of not having a cigarette for the next sixty seconds. "Gee, a whole minute of no cigarettes!" you think. "I can do that."

Over the first day or two, just consciously achieve this mini-goal. You'll find that you are in control of having a cigarette. The cigarette does not control you. You can make a conscious choice for at least sixty seconds.

A few days later, increase that conscious goal to two minutes or five minutes. Gradually build your personal control muscles and watch the nicotine addiction gradually fade.

After a week, set a goal of no cigarettes before 10 a.m. You're not making a lifelong goal here, just a goal from the time you wake up until 10 a.m. You can even cheat if you want to—just get up a little later in the morning, or even at 10 a.m.!

You can think, visualise, and perform short-term. So take advantage of this ability and break down your big goals into small, bite-sized goals.

### I WANT TO HAVE A BETTER, FRIENDLIER PERSONALITY

This is a popular goal. Most people would like to develop a friendlier, more outgoing personality.

Well, we could go out and start doing public speaking. For most of us, this would be a major, long-term goal. This would be extremely hard to achieve immediately, and would doom our goal to failure.

So let's break down this goal into miniature pieces and start with just one piece—compliments.

Our goal is to give one person, any person, a simple compliment today. Giving compliments is a great way to begin developing a friendlier personality. And you won't have to worry too much about rejection or hurting other people's feelings. People are so compliment-starved that the most common reaction to your compliment is shock! Compliment recipients may just freeze in place with their mouths open.

---

*You might try a few easy compliments, such as:*

"Nice car. I like the colour."
"What's that scent you're wearing?
It really smells great on you."
"Great suggestion. I'll put it to use right away."
"Thanks for the _____. It was very thoughtful of you."
"I like the way you arranged your desk."
"Cute dog. Does it do tricks?"

After a few days, you might try to accomplish your compliment-a-day goal before noon. After a week, increase your compliments to two a day.

See how easy it is? Small bites, little goals, 100% success.

What's next on my journey to a more pleasing personality?

Let's say that you like to correct people when they are wrong. This is a common activity people do. In fact, people do it with such gusto, you'd think they are getting paid to find fault with other people.

Anyway, you decide that you can allow people the freedom to indulge in their own opinions and viewpoints in life. It will be hard not to correct them with your perfect opinions and viewpoints, but you'll try.

You break down this big goal into a mini-goal of:

*I will not correct the first wrong viewpoint*
*or opinion I observe each day.*

That's it. Allow yourself the freedom to correct all the rest of the uninformed people you deal with that day. You don't want to overdo this good personality thing right away. You'd shock too many people!

Now, start your day and wait for the first wrong opinion or viewpoint. You shouldn't have to wait long; other people are so obliging. When you hear the first idiot opinion of the day, bite your tongue, face the other direction, roll your eyes, and ignore it. It will be hard, but you can do it.

After a few days, try to ignore two idiot opinions in a row. After a few months, maybe you'll be able to listen to illiterate conversations and just smile. You've achieved another step in your pleasing personality program.

## SMALL THINKERS ACHIEVE BIG GOALS

As you are building your goal achievement muscles, take the time to become a small thinker. While other people are dreaming about the big picture and never getting started, you're slowly, gradually building the goal achievement power that will take you anywhere you want to go.

At one of my goal seminars, I had a particularly small thinker sitting on the front row. He said:

"I want to lose weight, but I love to eat. Here's what I'm going to do. Starting today I'll eat my bread without butter. That's it. That's something I can easily do. I'm not addicted to butter. I just put it on bread out of force of habit, I guess. Since each pat of butter is about 100 calories, and I use three pats of butter a day, I'll be removing 109,500 calories over the next year. I'll be 30 pounds lighter this time next year!"

Small changes and small goals will add up to big achievements.

# The Psychology Of Goal Setting

The big problem most of us encounter when dealing with goals is that we're working with inaccurate information. In the past, we have made false assumptions about how to achieve goals based on wrong information. We're going to change all that.

---

### You'll soon learn:

- How we got this wrong information.
- Why goal setting works.
- How lists can change your life.
- Why professional victims shouldn't be reading this book
- What previously kept us from achieving our goals?
- Why focus makes goals happen.
- How goal-setters attract new prospects.

---

And this isn't all we'll learn. But, let's get started now. You don't want to wait any longer for a stress-free, goal achieving life, do you?

## ARE WE OPERATING ON WRONG INFORMATION?

Don't be shocked! But most of us are running our lives based on partially inaccurate information. How much of a difference can wrong information make?

Imagine you were sick and had an infection. Years ago, the accepted method of treatment was to slice open a vein and drain a lot of your blood. Yuck!

Well, today we know that's wrong information. Following that wrong information won't cure us and will most likely harm our health. Thank goodness someone was brave enough to try something different, or we'd all still be slicing veins open today.

Years ago, the accepted path to a comfortable life was to spend thousands of pounds and three years of your life at University. Then, you'd get hired by a major company and work 45 years until retirement. You would enjoy approximately three years of retirement before dying.

Today we'd laugh at such a scenario. After three years of University and thousands of pounds in accumulated debts, many University graduates still don't even have a job! And, if they do get a job, how long can they count on keeping it? Companies downsize, sell off divisions, close branch offices, merge, dissolve and basically make employees nomads. Today's employee can expect to bounce from company to company to company.

Yes, there's wrong information everywhere. If you don't think so, just listen to political campaign speeches.

## DOES SOME OF THIS WRONG INFORMATION RUB OFF ON US?

Of course. It's not hard to assimilate some of this wrong information into our lives. That's quite natural.

Remember, all the knowledge and information we have accumulated so far in our lives has made us what we are today. If we want to be more, have more, or share more, we're going to have to change and we can do this by setting new goals.

# Automatic Goal Setting Using Your Reticular Activating System

Setting goals is fun—especially if you believe you can achieve them. Let me tell you right up front that you were designed to be goal-orientated because you have a reticular activating system in your brain. The job of the reticular is to screen out everything that has no value to you. I demonstrate this at my seminars by asking the audience: "How many blue cars did you see on the way to this seminar?"

There is always a great hesitation at this point. They must have passed several dozen blue cars, but they can't recall noticing them.

I then say, "I really appreciate you coming to my seminars, so this is what I'm going to do you. On the way home tonight I want you to record the registration number of every blue car you see. Then just send me the list and I will pay you £5 for each number."

I watch their faces as they start to think of all the detours they can make so they have more opportunity to see more blue cars. Then the penny drops—blue cars had no value to them on the way to the seminar, so the reticular screened them out. On the way home, it was a different story; blue cars suddenly had value, so the reticular opened up and you would have seen hundreds—even if it meant driving round the block all night!

Having goals makes everything in the universe come to you, or so it seems. Like wanting to make spaghetti. Now, when you walk through the supermarket you notice how the pasta, sauce and other ingredients jump out at you because you need them. If you didn't have a goal, you would walk right past these ingredients. You would say there is no opportunity and drift through the store. With a goal, everything feels good, focused, directed and universally supplied, as you need it.

## MORE EXAMPLES OF HOW THE RETICULAR WORKS

Let's say that you walk into a tall 70-storey office building to visit a friend. You go through the lobby, take the elevator to the 34th floor, walk past the cafeteria, go through an open plan office maze, and eventually find your friend.

Now, what did you notice along the way?

Did you see the Christmas ornaments on the tree near the cafeteria?

No. They were unimportant. You were focusing on the path to your friend.

Did you see the calendar on one of the office cubicles as you walked by?

No. Your total focus was to meet your friend.

Did you notice all the different business names at the bottom of the elevators?

No. You already knew you were going to the 34th floor to see your friend.

Did you notice the signs that pointed to the toilets for men and women?

No. You wanted to go directly to your friend.

If your focus is going directly to your friend, then most of the information, people and opportunities you see along the way to your friend are ignored and unseen. You miss many opportunities and fail to take advantage of many things because you're totally focused on meeting your friend.

This is good!

If you allowed yourself to be distracted by everything you see along the way to your friend—well, you'll never get to your friend.

But, what if you wanted to go to the toilet...immediately?

Yes, after visiting with your friend, you go to the 34th floor's elevators and then...that Mexican dinner begins its toboggan ride through your system. The rumbling begins. The pressure builds. You feel like you'll soon explode! You tighten your stomach muscles to resist. Yes, you have an immediate need to find the toilet.

But uh, oh, you don't know where the nearest toilet is located. You didn't pay attention to the location of the toilets on the way to see your friend. Yes, there are plenty of toilets around, lots of opportunities, but you don't know where they are!

Why don't you know where they are?

Because you had a different goal when you passed the toilets, so you didn't recognise the opportunity.

You see, you must first have the goal, and then you'll recognise countless opportunities to fulfil that goal.

That's why clear-cut, focused goals are important. The goal tells your mind what opportunities to notice.

And what if you don't have a focused goal?

Then your mind doesn't focus on anything. You simply float through life missing millions of opportunities to achieve almost anything.

---

### No goal:
*No perception of opportunities.*

### Have a goal:
*Opportunities jump out at you by the hundreds.*

---

The opportunities in life are always there. You simply need a focused goal to see them.

Now, back to our rumbling stomach and our desperate panic to find the toilets.

What if you already knew that spicy jalapenos and Mexican food gave your stomach fits? When you finished your Mexican food, you knew that you'd be having a problem in just a few hours.

Will that change your attention? Will that motivate you to notice toilets wherever we go...just in case? I'm sure.

You know a Mexican food problem is coming. You want to be prepared. You're constantly noticing all the signs that point you to toilets.

On the way up to your friend on the 34th floor, what did you see?

First, you saw some toilet signs in the lobby next to the elevators. Next, you noticed the toilet signs when you left the elevator on the 34th floor.

There were toilets when you passed the cafeteria. You made special note of them as you heard your stomach make a little noise as you passed the display of food.

There also were toilets near the open plan office.

Yes, there were toilets everywhere, and you noticed all of them. You were focused and your mind took special note of all the toilet opportunities.

Opportunities are everywhere. We just have to notice them and that means having goals.

# Why Am I The Way I Am?

Your conscious mind is like a receiving station. It uses the five senses—sight touch, taste, smell and hearing—to record up to 70,000 bits of information every minute and stores this in the subconscious mind, never to be forgotten. And more importantly, it stores it as the *truth*. Your subconscious mind can be likened to the memory part of a computer and as such, the saying "garbage in, garbage out" is just as relevant.

As you go through life, you are constantly making decisions based on information that is stored in your subconscious mind. In fact it's this information that makes up your self-image—it's the truth about you.

*The image that you have of yourself today exists because of all the experiences you've had in the past; it has not made you the way you are—it's made you believe that you are the way you are.*

Remember that we make decisions based on past information that we store as the truth as we believed it to be—but is it always the truth or could we be making decisions based on wrong information? Absolutely we can, and I'll prove it to you.

### LET'S GET HUMBLE

Our first goal is to accept that we sometimes operate on wrong information. We fervently believe this information is correct, but it isn't.

Here is a simple but interesting exercise I do at my goal-setting seminars. I ask all the participants to take out a blank sheet of paper. Next, I ask them to draw a large square on one side of the paper. Then, I instruct them to dissect the square into four parts. Finally, I have them dissect each of the four parts into four additional parts.

The seminar participants are left with a drawing that looks like this:

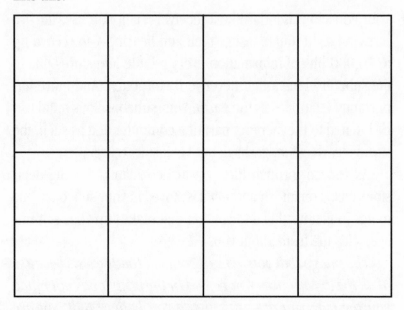

Once everyone is convinced they have the exact same drawing, I say the following: "Now, everyone take a close look at your drawing. Count how many squares you see in your drawing. You have fifteen seconds. When you have counted the number of squares on your drawing, write down your answer on the back of your page and hold up your answer above your head for everyone to see."

The participants count the squares, write down their answers and proudly hold up their pages. All of the participants firmly believe their answer is right.

Some participants write 16 squares as their answer. As they look around, they see that some people have 20 squares written as their answers. They think, "Boy, are those people dumb. They are probably the kind of people who make really bad decisions based on wrong information."

The people with 20 squares as their answer think, "Look at those idiots with 16 squares as their answers. No wonder they haven't achieved much in life. They can't see the big picture like we do."

A few participants have 24 squares written as their answer. They think, "It's obvious that we are the superior thinkers. We're natural-born leaders because we are smarter than the rest. If one of these lesser beings try to convince us that 24 squares are too much, we just won't listen to them."

Two or three participants have 26 squares as their answer. They think, "Wow! Good thing we took a bit of extra time to count all of the possibilities. We're not the type to operate on wrong information. That's what makes us different."

Finally, one person has 30 squares as his answer. He took the seminar before, so he knows the correct answer and is already operating on good information.

Occasionally there will be a few people with 32 or 36 squares as their answer. Double vision? Bad math skills? Good imaginations? I don't know.

The point of this exercise is to show participants that what they think is true, may not be true. And if you base your life on untrue information, you won't be satisfied with the results.

If you believe wrong information, and then act on wrong information, you will achieve the wrong results.

## MORE BAD INFORMATION

Twenty-five years ago most people believed that Wal-Mart was some junk dime store in Arkansas. They didn't believe in their future and didn't invest in their future. However, those that did invest in Wal-Mart are multi-millionaires today. Yes, Wal-Mart became the largest retailer in the world.

IBM was once a small company. What if you acted on the right information and invested in them 25 years ago? Would that few extra million pounds have made a difference in your life? I'll bet it would have.

People miss opportunities because they believe that franchises will never catch on, or that network marketing doesn't work. The opportunities are there, available for everyone, but you have to operate on the right information to take advantage of these opportunities.

As an example, let's go back in time, say a couple of thousand years. You've been invited to a business opportunity meeting. Your chariot's parked outside the amphitheatre and you're sitting there in your finest red silks under your freshly-polished breastplate. Your plume-decorated metal helmet is placed neatly between your bare knees and you wait patiently for the meeting to start. Finally the sharp-suited presenter stands up and introduces a new concept for cleaning your silk robes. Instead of the usual way of beating the silks with handfuls of twigs in the river he introduces a new concept called "Dry Cleaning." Not much has changed in two thousand years. Even then, a third of the audience were thinking that he should cut down on the fermented grapes at breakfast, another third thought he might be on to something but wanted to wait and see. Only a third recognised the potential and took action.

Are you willing to accept that taking no action will result in no change?

## FAITH, HOPE AND THE LOTTERY

Once there was a man down on his luck who had completely run out of options. His car was about to be repossessed. His mortgage was three months late and his dog had just chewed up his last good shoe. Suddenly, he saw a sign for the lottery. With what could only be a flash of divine inspiration, he felt

God must surely want him to play the lottery. Just one lucky number and millions of pounds would be his! His financial problems would be solved once and for all!

The drawing was scheduled for Saturday. He had five days to pray for divine intervention, so he did.

> *"Lord, help me win the lottery!"*
> *"Lord, help me win the lottery!"*
> *"Lord, help me win the lottery!"*

This went on and on, day and night till Saturday. That evening the number would be drawn and he would know if his prayers had been answered.

But at noon, his faith started to fail.

Looking up to heaven he said, "Lord, I've fasted and I've prayed. I've cried and I've begged. I've done everything I can, I hope You don't mess this up!"

Storm clouds started to gather and bolts of lightning suddenly struck near his feet. After recovering from his shock, a voice came from heaven and said:

"At least buy a ticket!"

## WHAT WOULD YOU DO WITH THE FOLLOWING OPPORTUNITY?

What if I came to your door selling lottery tickets for a noble cause? It costs £10 (not just a pound like the lottery tickets you can buy at the paper shops), and the first prize is only £1000. At first you balk. "Why spend £10 just to try to win £1,000?" you ask. Would you buy a ticket? After all, the pound lottery tickets promise you millions of pounds, even though the odds are 14,000,000 to 1. But what if I told you that this lottery has only one ticket to be sold and it's going to be sold to you?

"Hey, that's a guaranteed £990 profit! It's not like those rip-off lotteries everyone else plays! I'll take it!" you shout as you rip the ticket out of my hand and throw a £10 note in my direction. Maybe you'd beg to play the lottery again and again every week. You'd want me to call you every time I heard about one of these lotteries. You'd become my new best friend.

Well, there is such a "lottery." And you can play again and again, week after week—in fact, any time you want. And for every pound you invest in time, effort, learning, and hard work, you'll get back your money—sometimes one hundred fold!

You just have to buy the ticket.

"What ticket? Where can I get this guaranteed winner?"

Well, it's right between your ears if you know what you're looking for! Are you ready to accept that some of your information and beliefs may have to change for you to change?

## EVEN MORE BAD INFORMATION!

I give the following test during some of my seminars. Read the next sentence to your self and count the number of F's:

*Finished files in effect are the results of a few years of scientific study combined with the experience of many years of experts.*

Well—how did you do? Did you see 6 or 7 or 8 or even 9? If you did—well done. But read the sentence again and have a recount. Well, did you see more? Let's suppose tomorrow you go into work and your best friend said, "How many F's did you count?" You may say 6 or 7 or 8 or even 9. But if you didn't see 10 you would have gone through the rest of your life believing that there were less than 10 F's in that sentence. The truth is that there were 10 F's in that sentence and you read it at least twice!

Now do you understand how easily we can store wrong information, and then spend the rest of our lives making decisions based on that information? Remember your subconscious mind is non-judgmental. It doesn't know right from wrong, good from bad or true from false. It just stores information as the truth you believe it to be.

So, when people say, "I can't tell jokes, I can't sell, I can't get anybody interested in my Network Marketing business—is this the truth or is it only the truth as they believe it to be? You see, you don't have to stay the way you are—you can change by changing the information stored in your subconscious mind.

# Comfort Zones

Before I tell you how to reprogram your subconscious mind, you first need to understand comfort zones. Part of the job your subconscious mind does is to maintain your sanity by using comfort zones. In a nutshell, comfort zones reflect your self-image.

Let me tell you a story about little Johnny. Johnny was just eight years old when he started junior school. He was sitting happily enough in class although he wasn't taking much notice of what the teacher was saying. It all sounded pretty boring and soon he was drifting away daydreaming. Suddenly Johnny became aware that the teacher was talking to him; in fact, she was asking a question. Frantically, he wracked his brain, but for the life of him he had no idea what she was talking about. The teacher sensed that he had not been paying attention, so she decided to make an example out of him.

"Come out to the front of the class, Johnny, and explain to everyone what we've been discussing."

Johnny was horrified. He slowly rose from his chair and in a trance-like state made his way to the front of the class and turned to face them. By this time his mind had totally shut down, his systolic blood pressure was going through the roof, he was sweating and he could feel his little heart thumping in his chest.

For what seemed an age he just stood there, hating every second. Suddenly he was aware that all the class was laughing. They were pointing at him and giggling. His friend Elizabeth, who was sitting in the front row, said "Psst! Johnny! Your flies are open!"

Sure enough, as he slowly looked down he could see part of his shirt sticking out from the front of his short trousers. *Oh no!* he thought, as he went bright red with embarrassment. *This is the worst day of my life.*

Twenty years later as a young accountant his boss summoned him to explain to the board of directors the financial implications of a recent merger. I bet you can guess what happened. His only experience of talking in front of a group of people was that horrendous day twenty years ago. Immediately his subconscious creatively tried to avoid a rerun by physically making him feel sick. He started to sweat, his mind blanked, his blood pressure soared and his heart started to race. In a nutshell, he was right out of his comfort zone.

That's your body's way of physically protecting you. Every time you go to do something, your subconscious will either help or hinder you based on the experiences of the past.

To demonstrate this at my seminars I walk into the audience and ask for six volunteers to come up to the front and speak on the power of the subconscious mind for just sixty seconds. Generally, I have to pick them, so I carefully select the people who are avoiding my gaze and give them a number from one to six. They are usually looking down and shuffling their feet. (This is their comfort zones kicking in to creatively avoid the situation.)

Having chosen the six, everyone else starts to relax back into their comfort zones. I then announce that we won't start with number one, we'll start with number six and it's not the person I pointed to but the person on their right! The six new "volunteers" all experience mind blanks, their pulses start to race and their blood pressure goes through the roof. I have effectively put twelve people right out of their comfort zones!

Think of your comfort zones like central heating. Between 18 and 22 degrees Centigrade you're comfortable. Above or below that range, your subconscious goes into action and does what is necessary to keep you comfortable and in line with your self-image.

You don't even have to physically experience something in order for your subconscious to physically effect you. Your thoughts are enough.

Let me demonstrate what I mean. Imagine yourself at home and it's the middle of the night. You wake up feeling very thirsty. You slip out of bed and feel your way into the kitchen. You locate the fridge, open the door and by the light of the fridge you see a bright yellow lemon. You take the lemon, which feels cool and hard, over to the draining board where you cut it in half. It must be a very ripe lemon, because you see a fine mist of juice as you cut in to it. You take half the lemon in your hand, raise it to your mouth, and just as you sink your teeth into it, you squeeze it. The juice hits the back of your throat and you start to gag!

As you read, I suspect your saliva glands started to work overtime. Even though you didn't physically bite a lemon, your subconscious, based on past experiences, activated your saliva glands ready to dilute the citric acid. That's the power of the subconscious mind.

Your subconscious mind is remarkable in its ability to solve problems. You see it doesn't sleep. Your conscious mind shuts down but the subconscious continues to sift information and put it into a sort of filing system. That's why you can often go to sleep thinking about a problem and the next morning you wake up and the solution just pops into your head. The answer always seems so obvious, logical and simple so you smack your forehead and say to yourself, "Why didn't I think of that before?"

Another example of the power of the subconscious mind, and one which we've all experienced, is when we use it as an alarm clock. We go to bed saying, "I must wake up at six o'clock." You repeat this several times and *presto!* Right at six o'clock your eyes open, as if by magic.

Another important link between goal-setting and your mind is that you think in pictures. We are teleological in nature. If I were to mention the name Margaret Thatcher, you wouldn't see the letters M-A-R-G and so on. Instead, you see a picture of Mrs.Thatcher in your mind's eye. It's very important to understand that you cannot block the pictures if you hear the words. For example, if I was to say to you, "I do not want you to visualise....A bicycle!" There it is—you can't stop it.

Before we continue let's take a few moments to recap. I've explained that the conscious mind is like a receiving station using the five senses. It can take impressions and bits of information at the rate of 70,000 a minute. The subconscious mind is like a huge storage area—anything we've ever experienced is stored there as the truth and we record the act in accordance with the truth we believe it to be. The exercise with the F's shows us that we store information that is wrong, so we make decisions based on incorrect data.

But what does this have to do with goal-setting?

# Why Goal Setting Works

If you're with me so far, here is the secret—the reason why goal-setting works. Everyone would do it if they understood this secret.

When you look at a beautiful car, you see that car in your conscious mind. At the same time, your subconscious mind checks the picture of the car that you are driving now. If the two pictures are different, the subconscious mind will automatically do what ever is necessary to keep you driving your car. After all, this is the truth—you really do drive *this* car and it wants to keep you in your comfort zones.

Now suppose there was a way that we could fool the subconscious into believing that you are driving that beautiful car? The two pictures would be the same and you would still be in your comfort zones—until you get into your old car. Then the subconscious mind thinks to itself, "What are you doing driving this old Ford? You should be driving your beautiful car!" Remember the job of the subconscious is to maintain your sanity and keep you comfortable. It will then do whatever is necessary to make sure you drive that beautiful car.

Suddenly, people want to know about your Networking business. Your customers start to buy more products. You use more products. No's become yes's. Strangers become prospects. Everyone you introduce to your business wants to sign up immediately. And all this happens because your subconscious is now working for you rather than against you.

So how can we change the pictures in our subconscious mind so that they're the same as our conscious mind?

## FIRST CREATE THE EMOTION

Let's assume you dream about owning a black Mercedes soft top. You go down to the local dealer and secure a test drive. The first thing you notice is the wonderful smell of the soft leather upholstery. The door closes with a reassuring, heavy clunk and the engine's so quiet that you have to look at the tachometer just to make sure that it's still running! You glide out of the garage forecourt and marvel at the feel of the power steering. The 8-speaker surround sound system fills the car with beautiful, clear music, and as you press the accelerator you feel the car respond instantly, pressing your back into the leather-bound, orthopaedically-designed seat.

As you cruise along familiar roads you can't help but notice the admiring glances the car is getting. Then, just as you think life can't get any better, you spot your useless brother-in-law who scoffed at your business presentation and told you it would never work. You lean on the horn just to make sure he sees you. As you wave to him you can't help but notice the look of disbelief as he recognises you. A glance in the rear view mirror confirms that he's stopped in his tracks. His eyes are open really wide and his jaw has dropped several inches! Yes, life doesn't get much better than this.

All too soon your test drive is over. As you park on the forecourt and return the keys, you experience a strong emotional tie to that car—but is it really the car that you want? Think about it and you will probably come to the conclusion that it isn't. After all, what is your favourite car? Nothing more than a bit of metal, some wood and rubber. So why do we get so excited about owning our dream car? Well, the answer is very simple—it's the emotion we feel when we drive it! The key to goal-setting is to experience your goals so you feel the emotions. But how?

## WORDS TRIGGER PICTURES
## THAT BRING ABOUT EMOTIONS

Words, pictures and emotions all make an impression on your subconscious mind, but it's the emotions that have the biggest effect. In terms of percentages, words would be about 10%, pictures 30% and emotions 60%.

By first experiencing our goals and then using words and pictures to remind us of the product or event, we are constantly feeling the emotions. By looking at and feeling the emotions several times a day, the information (which you automatically convert into pictures) overrides existing information in your subconscious. When the two pictures are the same, your subconscious mind will automatically go into action and assist you in doing whatever is necessary to make your pictures a reality—without you even realising it.

## AFFIRMATIONS

A simple but very effective way to do this is through affirmations, or what some people call *pre-determined self talk*.

Get some 3x5 cards and write down your goals, one on each card. It's very important to write the affirmation in the present tense, as if you had achieved it already! Remember that your subconscious mind is non-judgmental. As I explained, it does not know the difference between right or wrong, good and bad, true or false. It just stores information.

Let's look at a few examples.

"I really enjoy driving my black soft-top Mercedes and love to see people admiring it."

Notice I use emotional words like *enjoy, love* and *admire*. Now the best times to read your affirmations are just before you go to sleep and first thing in the morning. Read the first card, then close your eyes and see the pictures in your mind's eye, then feel the emotions you got from driving the car.

Let's try another.

"I now weigh nine stone and fit comfortably into a size 12. I look terrific and my friends keep complimenting me on my figure. I'm really looking forward to wearing a bikini this summer."

I hope you're getting the picture. Just read the words, visualise the affirmation, and let the emotions sweep over you.

A good tip is to position these pictures around your home —say on the bathroom mirror or the fridge. Make sure you have copies by your bed, so that last thing at night and first thing in the morning, you can look at your goals and feel the emotions. This is the best time to do goal-setting!

Wouldn't it be wonderful to be able to use this power to achieve anything you wanted out of life? And the good news is, you can! Unfortunately, most people misuse it. Remember it's non-judgmental. It works just as well at holding us back as it does pushing us forward to achieving our full potential. It's your decision. You don't have to stay the way you are; you can change—just like I did some twenty years ago when I learned the secret of making lists!

# The Lists That Can Change Your Life

Here are the techniques that changed my life and which can change yours, too. The most important thing I learned to do was write lists.

I'm sure that sounds simplistic, but it's important to know which lists you need and how to use them. That's where most people go wrong. After all, do you think that before my first seminar I didn't know how to write a list? Though I was a surveyor in the British Army, I was not *that* dumb! Probably, I'm like a lot of people. I went away and I analysed what I'd learned at the seminar. And I spent night after night analysing the tapes and all my notes and my wife's notes, as well. Gradually, I put it into a system that I could really understand and use, and I hope it has the same affect on you as it did on me.

## DEFINE YOUR IDEAL LIFESTYLE

First of all, it's very important to understand where you are right now, and where you want to be for the rest of your life. Goals that are meaningful enough to motivate us to action usually involve a vision of where we want to be—a picture of the future.

Call it a dream list, a vision list or whatever, but your first list should be your picture of the future—in other words, "defining your ideal lifestyle." Write down all the things that you would like to happen so that you can live your ideal lifestyle. In your dream list, assume no limitations to your talent, time or income. What could you accomplish if there were no limits to your time, talent, and income? What would you really, *really* want to do? Sunbathe 180 days straight while sipping an exotic drink on the deck of the Queen Elizabeth ocean liner? Climb Mt. Everest? Find a cure for cancer? Sail a 116-foot yacht around the world on your own?

When we first wrote our dream list, Anne wanted to go clothes shopping and buy designer dresses without looking at the sleeve to see how much it cost. I wanted to go to expensive restaurants and order food without looking at the right-hand column where the prices were printed. What would you really, *really* like to do?

## CREATE YOUR IDEAL LIFESTYLE

Now that you have a list of things that "seem impossible," you must take action to create your ideal lifestyle. It's time to make a second list, your goal list.

What's the difference between a dream list and a goal list? Goals are stepping stones you take towards achieving your ideal lifestyle. Each stepping stone has a time limit. Some you can achieve in a week, others may take several months or even years. They are often talked about in terms of short-, medium- or long-term goals.

- If your dream is to find a cure for cancer and you've just finished medical school, you probably won't do that this year. But you can read 20 research papers on cancer.

- If your dream is to cruise the world on the QE 2, you might at least have as your goal to open a "world cruise savings account" and have £1000 in there in twelve months.

- If your dream is to own a driving school with 17 cars and you still take the bus everywhere yourself, your goal might be to get a safe and reliable used car for you to start learning to drive.

- If your dream is to become a network marketing millionaire, perhaps your goal for this week ought to be to sign the distributor application and buy some products!

## STEPPING STONES TO SUCCESS

Each of your goals is like a journey, and the successful completion of a goal is like arriving at your destination. Each journey can be broken down into a number of objectives or steps that have to be taken in order to reach your goal. Each step or objective has to be clearly defined and completed within your time frame.

As an example, think of Sir Edmund Hillary. He didn't walk past Mt. Everest and decide to climb it one sunny afternoon! When he reached the summit, it was the culmination of months of planning in terms of equipment, oxygen, clothing, routes, personnel, guides, food, fitness and a million and one other things. He successfully achieved a huge goal by meticulously planning all the objectives and then achieving them step-by-step within a certain time frame. Your success in Life is no more than the methodical accomplishment of a number of small achievable steps. After all, "How do you eat an Elephant? One bite at a time!"

Once you know what your goals are, you then have to attach a monetary value that you will focus on day and night. This number will be what you want to earn each month from your network marketing business on top of what you presently earn. It's the amount that will enable you to achieve your smaller goals—for example, eating out more, taking the family away for the weekend or buying a new hi-fi.

It has to be a number that gets you excited, an amount of income that motivates you to do network marketing. You have to believe that if you achieve that figure, you will be able to achieve the goals that it was set for.

So starting at £200 per month, think about your goals and whether this amount really gets you excited. If it doesn't, then move up in increments of £100. The key is to get a monthly figure that really makes you *want* to do network marketing, because this number will motivate you to start achieving your short-term goals. It doesn't stop there, because once you consistently achieve that figure, you increase it again until it fires you up to achieve some of your medium-term goals—for example, a family holiday to Disneyworld, or a new car, or even a house extension.

Your long-term goals will probably include financial independence. This simply means that you can do what you like when you like with whom you like. It means getting out of bed when you're tired of sleeping. It means being free of the JOB, which for most of us is an abbreviation for being "Just Over Broke." Employers are notorious for paying you just enough to stop you from leaving. It means that every month a cheque from your network marketing company drops on your mat along with all the bills. It means that you can pay all those bills and, before you can spend what's left, *another* cheque arrives....

# The Secret List

Perhaps you're saying, "I already know all this!" That may be true, but I'll wager you don't know about my secret list. It's a list that I've rarely heard about elsewhere, but it makes all the difference. I call it the value list.

Every network marketer has been told to have a dream list and for the most part they went home and wrote down what they wanted to have. Some network marketers even went home and wrote out a goal list and wrote down what they wanted to achieve. But almost none have sat down and decided what they wanted to *be!* Now it's time for you to decide what you want to be and what things are supremely important to you in this life.

- Do you want to be a great speaker and help people change their lives?

- Do you want to be a great mother or father, the kind your children will never forget?

- Do you want to be a great recruiter who makes other people successful and secure?

Just what do you value more than anything else? Money? Security? Family? Freedom? Fame? Health? Respect? Friendships? Know what it is and be honest about what you really want to be.

Once you write out a value list, compare it to your goal list and your dream list. They must "match up" for you to succeed. Many people try to achieve goals that are incompatible with their personal values. It's a bit like swimming against the tide. So you need to check for consistency.

If your most important value is to become famous, then you could achieve this by finding a cure for cancer. However, if your goal is to finish a car mechanic's course in the next few months instead of medical school or biology school, you might have a conflict there. Car mechanics don't generally cure cancer. On the other hand, if you're going to pay your way through medical school by fixing cars at mechanic's wages instead of working for minimum wages, your goals, values and dreams really could be consistent. But it's your job to be absolutely sure!

Or if your supreme value is being the best mother possible, and your dream is to stay at home with your children, but your immediate goals are to work the midnight shift at the factory, be President of the school Parent Teacher Organisation, and go back to college part time, you might be too tired to be the mother you want to be. Something has to give!

And it goes without saying, if you want to be the Pope, your first goal, men, should *not* be to get married!

If you've been honest about your values, they will win out every time. You will change your goals and dreams to live out your values every time!

## YOU CAN'T CHANGE PEOPLES' VALUES

The best favour you can do for yourself or someone in your downline is to help them be honest about their deepest values. That's why we do the value list last. We let people air out all their noble-sounding dreams and goals, and then we see if they're consistent with what makes this person *really* tick.

Some people in your downline will realise they only want to purchase products. Maybe their life's calling is to go back to school and be a nursery school teacher. But others will know that it's in their best interest to pursue your business opportunity all out and will get serious!

Not knowing what we value most is the reason why we have so much dead wood in network marketing. People say they want a new car, have a goal to start a new business, or any number of high sounding goals and dreams, but secretly they value drinking beer on the settee, watching TV and hoping someone will bring them food!

Want to know an excellent training tip? Instead of convincing people to have different values, just work with the people whose values are compatible with your network marketing business! Or talk to them when their values change on their own. But don't try to change their values for them.

Now, back to you. Have you re-drawn your goal list? Does your dream list truly reflect what you value? Have you made your stated goals consistent with what you truly want to be? That is the best way to achieve your stated goals without having your goals 'mysteriously' change and making you constantly feel defeated.

Now we've hopefully made your dream list, your goal list and your value list consistent. If this is true, your deepest motivations will constantly drive you on to success...if the path between your values and dreams is realistic.

So how do you go about making your goal list realistic? Answer: your Action Plan.

---

**Whenever possible,**
1. Choose small, short term goals that can be chipped away at daily, instead of monster goals, and
2. Choose an activity goal instead of a results goal.

Instead of having the immediate goal of 10,000 people in your downline, which could happen in one year or more, choose a goal of having ten people in your downline, which could happen in as little as a month or even a week.

Instead of saying, "My goal is to recruit one person per day," set a goal that is based on something you can control. You can't control whether people will sign up, but you *can* control your activity. Sometimes ten presentations will mean ten sign-ups. At other times, ten presentations will mean zero response. All you can control is your activity: talking to people. So focus on that. Instead of having the goal of signing up one person per day, have the goal of talking to three new people per day about your business. Some days three people will sign up. Other days you'll be fortunate to get anyone to even listen to your audiocassette. But if you spoke with three people, you'll have still met your goal and reinforced the habit of success!

If you could speak with three new people daily about your business, and teach your new distributors to do the same thing, your income worries would be gone soon enough! Speaking with three new people per day is challenging, yet completely possible. Talk to enough people and you'll find plenty of folks who want what you have to offer. Yet, even if people say "no" until you perfect your skills, you're still creating habitual success instead of failure. Soon, meeting hundreds of small goals will snowball and you'll find yourself wondering why success seemed so difficult in the first place!

### YOUR DAILY ACTIVITY LIST

To keep you on track and maintain momentum, you need to have a daily activities list. This list is compiled so that you can priorities the activities that will move you towards achieving each step of your goal.

The secret here is the word *priorities*. Remember that 80% of the results you wish to achieve in the day are produced by just 20% of your work! Time is your most precious commodity.

**"IF YOU FAIL TO PLAN, YOU PLAN TO FAIL!"**

These are the lists that can change your life as they did mine. Now it's your turn to start using them:

---

**1.** Write your lists now.
**2.** Check for consistency between each of your values-dreams-goals.
**3.** Rewrite your goals and dreams as needed
**4.** Make sure your goals are small and attainable to quickly establish a habit of success.

---

Supposing you had a bank that credited your account each and every morning with £86,400, and every evening cancelled whatever part of the amount you had failed to use during the day, what would you do? Draw out every penny of course!

Well, you have such a bank and its name is Time. Every morning it credits you with 86,400 seconds. Each night it rules off, as if lost, whatever of this you have failed to invest to good purpose. It carries over no balances. It allows no overdrafts. Each day it opens a new account with you. Each night it burns the records of that day. If you fail to use the day's deposits the loss is yours. There is no drawing against tomorrow. You must live in the present—on today's deposit invest it so as to get from it the utmost in health, happiness and success!

I'm often asked the question, "Which goals are more important the short-, medium- or long-term. It's a very good question because each has its merits. But if pressed I would opt for long-term goals. Think of walking along a railway line. If you were looking down at your feet and taking care to slowly place each of your steps on the rail. You would probably wobble quite a bit. As you extended your gaze to say ten to fifteen metres in front of you, your balance and speed would improve. If you continued to look even further down the line, your balance and speed would improve even more.

So yes, I think long-term goals are the most important, but even better would be if you were able to share those goals with someone. Imagine that partner walking alongside you. If you both extended an arm so your fingertips just touched, you could walk together—forever.

# You Can Talk Yourself Into Anything You Want!

You have a mind that is simply amazing. Let me demonstrate what I mean. Let's say you're walking down the street and you see your boss coming towards you. You stop, shake hands and exchange a few pleasantries. You decide to ask your boss for some time off, but just as you start to ask, your conscious mind gets a message from the subconscious mind telling you to STOP! The communication goes something like this—

*Conscious mind:* "What's up?"

*Subconscious:* "We are taking impressions at the rate of 70,000 a minute and we can tell from the slant of his head, the look in his eyes, the humidity, his posture, the clothes he's wearing—in fact, his whole body language is telling us that if you continue to ask the question you will get a negative reply."

*Conscious mind:* "Terrific. There's only one problem: I've already got the first four words out of my mouth!"

*Subconscious:* "No problem! We've taken those four words, run them through the computer down here and come up with five sentences that start with those same four words but have nothing to do with time off."

*Conscious mind:* "Terrific, but I only need *one* sentence."

*Subconscious:* "No problem. We've run those five questions through the computer and come up with the best sentence using those first four words and the fifth word is...!"

You achieved that thought process in the time it takes you to snap your fingers and I know you've experienced this amazing power many times during your life.

Experts tell us that we only use 2% of our mind's potential. It should come as no shock to you now that if we use our minds to work for us, instead of against us—then all things are possible.

# Goals Attract Followers

You're lost in the middle of the Sahara desert. It's so bad that not even the British Army goes there (until they read this book at least). It's not a pleasant experience. It's hot, you're thirsty and you're tired of the sand dune scenery. A hot bath, a cup of tea, and an aeroplane ticket home sound just fine. If only you could get to civilisation.

A group of nomads approaches you. Frantically, you wave to them and stop their caravan. The leaders says, "Hey, what are you doing out here?"

You answer, "I'm lost, terribly lost. I'd like to go with you if I could. By the way, where are you going?"

The nomad caravan leader says, "Going where? We are already here. We're nomads. We simply travel the desert. In fact, I've been roaming the desert since I was born. So, where are we going? I don't know, but we'll arrive there tomorrow or next week or next month."

You politely say farewell to the leader and decide to wait for the next caravan.

The next day, a new caravan comes along. Again, you run up to the caravan's leader and say, "Where are you going?"

The leader answers, "We're on our way to Casablanca. We will arrive on the 4th. Next, we take the traders' route to Algiers. We arrive in Algiers on the 22nd and pick up new camels. Then, it's onward to Tunisia for the annual camel rodeo. Would you like to come along?"

"You bet!" you reply. Finally you can follow someone who knows where he is going. Now you're on your way to civilisation, a hot bath, a cup of tea and that flight home.

When you want to achieve a goal in your life, who do you follow? The person who is lost and unfocused? Or, do you prefer following the leader who knows where he is going?

It's obvious. If we want to get somewhere, let's follow somebody who knows where he is going.

And that focused leader can be you!

That's right. If you have focused goals, know where you are going and how to get there, the world will crowd around you and ask to join you on your journey. You will literally attract people to you because you know where you are going.

The world is full of followers, people desperate for some direction in their lives. These people stand in awe of the few leaders who realise they can choose their own goals and direction. Once you decide where you are going, you'll be one of those rare beacons that the uniformed world flocks to. It's almost unbelievable that so few people will set their own goals in life. Most of the people are content to observe your goals, and decide to come along for the ride.

Will this have any effect on your network marketing business? Absolutely!

Once your natural market of contacts learn that you have a focused goal, a direction in your life, many of them will decide to come to you for guidance and leadership. If you independently decide that you want more financial freedom in your life, here is what happens:

> A couple of co-workers say, "Hey! That's a good idea. I thought we were sentenced here for life. We'd like to come along with you and build a part-time business, too!"
>
> Your neighbour says, "Wait a minute. If you're going to be making some part-time extra income, don't leave me out. Let me in on your secret."
>
> A cousin calls you and says, "I heard you're going to build a full-time business and leave your job. I don't like my job much, either. Could you tell me how this works?"

The Magic of Goal Setting

A prospect you invite to the business opportunity meeting says, "I like where this opportunity can take me. I want to join you and make this business successful for me and my family."

See the difference your personal goals and direction make in other people's lives? They'll become willing prospects for your network marketing opportunity when they see you leading the way.

So, should you keep your goals secret and hidden from the rest of the world? Or, should you share your goals and dreams and help others who are desperately looking for someplace to go?

# If I'm A Goal Achievement Machine, Why Do I Fail To Accomplish Some Of My Goals?

You don't fail to achieve the unfulfilled goals that you have set. You simply changed your goal.

What? *Changed* my goal?

Yes, you simply substituted a different goal and gave that new goal a priority.

For example, let's say that you set a goal to attend this evening's business opportunity meeting. When you arrive home, you're tired, frustrated with traffic, hungry, and you find out that your neighbour has a spare ticket for the International at Wembley tonight. What do you do?

You change your goal. You make a new goal of attending the big game with your neighbour. And if you're lucky, you'll achieve that new goal and have a great time.

No, you didn't fail to achieve your original goal of attending the business opportunity meeting, you simply changed the goal because there was something else you wanted more. That's human nature. That's life. Don't be upset that you changed goals, as it happens all the time. Since we are in charge of our own lives, why shouldn't we set the goals that will make us happy?

We just have to be mature enough to realise the consequences of changing our goals. In the future, we can reminisce about watching that big soccer match. We can also regret not bringing a guest to that business opportunity meeting.

### TELEVISION IS MORE FUN THAN REJECTION

Let's say that you set a goal to personally telephone or contact three new prospects every day. You want to build your business fast so this activity is very important to you. Now remember, you'll set a goal to achieve whatever is important to you.

After making the first two personal contacts, you feel destroyed because these prospects dumped all their negative feelings on you. They didn't spare anything. They told you how bad their lives were, how awful it was that you interrupted their miserable lives, how they curse the day you came into their lives and tried to change their lives, how inconsiderate you were to contact them, and so on. These first two contacts were so depressing and the rejection so personal that you are devastated. So what do you do?

You set a new goal to watch television.

You decide that watching television is more pleasurable than the bitter rejection you experienced with these first two prospects. You decide that avoiding rejection is more important to you than achieving financial success in your network marketing business. That's okay if that is what you want. Just make sure you realise that you are making this choice.

Once you realise that you are the one who sets the goals, almost any possibility in life becomes available to you. You'll achieve the goals you set. Just stay focused so that your goals won't change.

Now, what if I had told you that by not going to the soccer match and attending the business opportunity meeting instead, you'd have been able to sponsor someone who would end up helping your organisation earn an additional £10,000 per month? What do you want more? A night at the big match or month after month of extra money?

Most of us would choose the latter. The only problem is that there are no guarantees that you'd sponsor anyone by missing the big match, let alone a heavy hitter. That's why it's probably OK to change your goal...once in a while.

Check yourself, though. Are you changing your goals all the time? If so, you really need to ask, "What do I *really* want?"

The answer to that question is: whatever you're willing to work for.

## Professional Victims

I was waiting in line for lunch on the top deck of a beautiful cruise ship. When cruising, all your meals are free. This would be happiness for almost anyone, except that fat person in front of me. He hated waiting in line. The two-minute wait was almost intolerable. He told me:

"The lobster last night at dinner was too dry. I forced myself to order the filet mignon, but I really wanted lobster. I don't know what the staff is going to do about this, but I'm not happy. It ruined my evening. And if that wasn't bad enough, the music was too loud at the entertainment last night, too. You'd think they would consider that most of us don't like loud music. The staff here is pompous, inconsiderate, and incompetent. I can't believe I paid good money for this kind of treatment."

Oh, dear! I was having a *great* time. I didn't realise things were this bad. I looked around and everyone else seemed to be having a good time, too. We all ate the same meals and attended the same entertainment. I guess most people enjoyed themselves because they chose to enjoy themselves.

The man ahead of me in the lunch line chose not to enjoy himself. I imagine that if the staff personally brought him a freshly-caught lobster and presented him with personalised earplugs to muffle the loud music...well, I'm sure he would have found something else to complain about!

#### WE ARE AS HAPPY AND SUCCESSFUL AS WE CHOOSE TO BE

When we choose a goal and stay focused, then our goal becomes reality. The rest of the cruise passengers and I chose a goal of having a great time.

What happened to us? We had a great time.

Oh sure, a few things did go wrong for us, too—but we stayed focused on our goal of having a great time. If the mashed potatoes were cold, we'd simply enjoy the hot apple pie for dessert. By focusing on our long-term goal of having a great time, we were able to see past these little bumps in the road.

I felt sorry for the negative fat man in the line in front of me. Maybe he didn't know that he had a choice, whether to be happy or sad, successful or unsuccessful, or to become physically fit or a physical wreck. This man probably felt he had no choices and that he was subject to the will and desires of everyone else in the world.

## WE CALL THESE PEOPLE PROFESSIONAL VICTIMS

Why? Because they always blame others for the bad things that happen in their lives. They believe they can't control their own lives. They are convinced that their feelings and moods are controlled by service clerks, other motorists, spouses, children, and actors on the television. They are just victims of other peoples' actions.

These professional victims feel that they are the ping-pong balls of life: everyone knocks them around and their whole life is just a reaction to other people's actions. They are unable to choose a personally-directed action. That's for other people to do. They can only react to their environment.

Unfortunately, these professional victims don't limit their appearances to cruise ships. They will also congregate around your network marketing business. Let's listen to a professional network-marketing victim:

"Of course I'm not happy. I work just as hard as my sponsor, Mary, yet she gets all

the breaks. Sure, she goes to all the opportunity meetings and trainings, but I would,
too, if I could sponsor the same good distributors that she does. This networking
business is unfair. Our company just doesn't
play fair. The compensation plan is too hard.
The products are overpriced. I don't see
how anyone can make a living here. Whenever a good prospect becomes available,
the prospect joins my sponsor, not me. I
don't understand why. Some people get all
the breaks. Am I happy? No. I'll become
happy and successful in my network marketing business when the world decides to
change. In the meantime, I'll be miserable
until things start to go my way."

Well, this professional victim is going to have a long wait to
see if the world is going to conform to his dream. And it's
going to be a long, *long* time before a prospect chooses this
victim as a sponsor instead of Mary, the lady that goes to meetings, gives trainings, and is positive about the business.

# Do You Have Some Professional Victims In Your Group?

You know who they are. They're the ones who think there is a conspiracy of outside influences that keep them from being successful.

They're easy to spot. Just listen to their identification calls:

"Oh, I can't be successful...
  —because the home office lost my order."
  —because the company didn't work."
  —because the marketing plan doesn't work."
  —because the products cost too much."
  —because the products cost too little."
  —because my sponsor lives too far away."
  —because the staff were rude to me."
  —because my friends aren't interested."
  —because I don't know anyone."
  —because everyone said 'no.'"
  —because it is too hard."
  —because it takes too long to make money."
  —because the company should pay for my training."
  —because I shouldn't have to pay for sales aids."
  —because I don't know how and don't want to learn."
  —because I need money now."
  —because I don't have any money."
  —because advertising doesn't work."
  —because I don't want to stock products."
  —because I can't think of any other excuses."

What's the common denominator in all of these excuses? Easy. It's the person giving us the excuses. If we handle one excuse, the person will quickly jump to another excuse.

Professional victims believe that success lies outside of themselves. They don't see themselves as capable of success. They believe that they must find the perfect opportunity, and that the perfect opportunity will work really hard all by itself (while they watch from a distance), and that perfect opportunity will make them rich.

That's some pretty far-fetched logic.

The professional victims in network marketing spend their careers jumping from one program to another, looking for that perfect opportunity that will make them rich. Because they never work any program, every program they join fails to make them rich.

What can you do to break this vicious cycle of professional victim thinking?

Not much.

The victims won't let you change them. You can't change them because you want them to change. The only way for professional victims to change is for them to *want* to change. Unfortunately, that's pretty rare.

So, what are your options as a leader?

**1.** Become a missionary, a psychologist, a supreme humanitarian with a life's purpose of tending to the professional victims who don't want to change. You can whisper positive affirmations in their ears, conduct long psychoanalysis sessions on leather sofas, follow them around with a tape recorder that plays positive subliminal tapes, show uplifting videos on their TVs, yell power phrases to shock them into awareness. Who knows? After 20 or 25 years you might accomplish a breakthrough and get one victim to reconsider the options. That's a long, long wait for a maybe.

**2.** Or, you can simply allow the professional victims to quietly retire from your network marketing business, and wish them luck in their search for a new career that will require no personal responsibility.

Since most leaders have limited time, we have to donate our time to people who want help, who want assistance, and who want to progress in their own network marketing career. We can't afford to minister to the professional victims and ignore the working distributors who need our help.

### A FINAL WORD OF CAUTION

If you personally complain a lot, if you are a professional victim, if you are easily influenced by other people, if you are scared of everything, then *please* don't even consider network marketing. If you expect the company to make you successful, if you expect your sponsor to make you successful, and if you expect your mum to fix things and make life fair, then please, *please* don't get involved in network marketing. You will most definitely have a bad experience.

You will probably be happier in a government job that promises no stress, no work, no quotas, and cradle-to-grave job security. Now this isn't such a bad choice, and the only price you'll have to pay is your dreams. If you can afford to give up your dreams, then polish up your resumé, apply for that government job and enjoy life.

However, if you choose to surrender your dreams to avoid taking personal responsibility for your life and personal responsibility for your accomplishments, please don't look back on your life with regret and say, "There is so much I could have done, if I had only tried."

## "I Can't Be Happy And Successful When Things Aren't Right"

Professional victims say: "I don't have the power to decide if I can be happy or sad. I'm merely a puppet on a set of strings controlled by other people and events. If they pull a string, my left arm must go up. Or, if they pull a different string, my right leg must go up. I have no choice. Other people and things determine if I'm going to be happy or sad."

Is it impossible to be happy when things aren't right?

Look around.

You see some people happy and some people sad, yet both groups experience the same world.

For instance, when two teams play for the championship, one group of people will be happy with the result, and the other group will be sad. Yet, both groups of people observed the same game. Do you think that the difference is that people chose their individual reaction to the game?

Two people watch the same musical. One person enjoys the experience and raves about the musical to his friends. The other person complains that the music was uninspiring, the seats were too crowded, and the stage settings boring. This person bitterly complains that he spent money to attend such a travesty.

Yet, both people attended the same musical. Was it the musical that made one person happy and the other person sad? Or, did these people choose their reactions to the same musical?

Two people attend an opportunity meeting. One person leaves in disgust. "The hype and excitement is too phoney. Nobody will ever buy those products," he says. "Looks like a pyramid to me. You've got be a super salesman to be successful in that business."

The other attendee says, "Wow! Word-of-mouth networking is the marketing method of the future. It's time I get in on it. It makes sense that people would buy from friends, people they trust, instead of some anonymous corporate store. My friends will want to take advantage of this financial opportunity, too!"

Same opportunity meeting. Two different reactions. Did these people choose their reactions?

What about a young married couple in London who have money problems? They live in an average flat with kitchen appliances and a television. They can't afford a car. They can't afford to go to restaurants to eat. They can't afford new clothes. Creditors call them on the telephone. The couple are unhappy and miserable.

Yet, does their situation make them miserable, or do they simply choose to be miserable?

What about another young married couple in Jamaica? They don't have an average apartment. Their living quarters are with the spouse's parents. They don't have a television or a car. They can't afford to eat at restaurants or buy new clothes. Creditors can't call them because they don't even own a telephone. Yet this couple are extremely happy.

Does their situation make them happy, or do they simply choose to be happy?

So what's the good news?

The good news is that happiness and success are inside jobs.

Happiness and success are not controlled by outside conditions. That's good, because we can't control outside events and other people. Thankfully we don't have to be happy or sad depending on somebody else's mood or actions. It's human nature to want to change our outside conditions, but fortunately we don't have to change anything on the outside to be happy or successful.

## THE TIME FOR CHANGE IS NOW

In my Army days, most Mondays would start with a brew up. When everyone had a mug of tea the post week-end whinging and whining would start. We would blame the weather, the football results, the Government, the job, the wife—in fact, nothing was safe from our wrath. We blamed everything for our lack of success in life. We were standing around waiting for something to happen that was going to change our lives. Unhappy, unsuccessful people want change in their life. However, they don't personally want to change. They want the world to change. So, they believe: "I'll be happy just as soon as the world changes everything and configures itself to my whims and needs."

I was unhappy, unsuccessful, but then I finally looked in the mirror and saw the problem: it was me. It had nothing to do with weather, the Government or the job. It was me.

First, I had to change, and then everything around me would change.

If happiness and success are controlled by what's *inside* us, then this is something we can control. All we have to do is personally change ourselves or how we look at the outside world to be happy and successful.

It's obvious to everybody but the professional victim that the place for change is within ourselves. We attract our success, and we also attract our failure. It's up to us to design ourselves so that we control what we attract.

## WE BECOME LIKE THE PEOPLE WE ASSOCIATE WITH

Hang around with the grumps and you become a grump; hang around with dynamic, exciting people and you become a dynamic, exciting person. When I finally realised this I started reading books like *The Magic of Thinking Big*, *You Can Become the Person You Really Want to Be*, and *How to Win Friends and Influence People*. I started hanging around with successful people. I watched the way they walked , how they smiled, how they shook hands, the kind of clothes they wore— and copied them.

Still not convinced? Then why are we always trying to protect our children from little Johnny up the road who swears, smokes, and is always in trouble with the police? Answer: We know that if our children associate with Johnny, the chances are they will copy him. Isn't it sad that we forget this simple rule of human nature as we become adults?

## WHY IS THIS SUCH A SECRET?

Because people don't want to change themselves. They don't want to take personal responsibility for their own lives. It's just easier to blame your spouse, your boss, your neighbour, your dog, the weather, the television, the car or the traffic. They see change as something other people should do.

Are people ready to change? No.

If our professional victim changes himself to become a more positive person, won't he attract more distributors to his organisation? Of course.

Do people see the relationship between changing what they do and the results they get? No. They can't see how their actions create the results in their lives.

The game of life is our competition. There are plenty of uninformed people who are waiting for something to happen. That's why anybody who attempts to make something happen soars above the crowd with amazing speed.

Do something.

Do anything.

And watch the results follow.

# Cause And Effect

No one seems to argue about cause and effect. We accept this truth, but do we really use this truth to our advantage?

---

## Everyone would agree that:

- If you step off tall buildings, the result will be an accelerated free fall, straight down.

- If you drink extremely hot coffee, you will burn your tongue.

- If you run as fast as you can for five minutes, you'll run out of breath.

- If you eat large quantities of high-fat foods, you will get fat.

---

### EVERY ACTIVITY WILL PRODUCE A RESULT

That is what cause and effect means. Cause and effect is a universal law. It's something we expect. In fact, we'd be quite surprised if we stepped off a tall building and just floated in mid-air. This is a universal law: when we perform a certain activity, then we should expect a certain result.

But what if you don't like the result? How do you change it? To get a different result, you must *change* the activity. To get a different effect, you need a different cause.

Remember my jog in Kenya's lion country? That's where I first recognised this principle. If I didn't want to get eaten, it was best to head back to camp pronto and change my activity.

Jogging in lion country was a cause whose effect I didn't want to experience!

Let's say that every time you step off that tall building, you fall to the pavement and hurt yourself. After doing this exercise three or four times, you decide that you want a different result. You're tired of hurting yourself.

What do you do? You don't go to the top of the building anymore. Instead, you walk into the first floor restaurant of the building and order a pizza.

Now you're going to have a different result.

It's easy. Different activity, different result.

It sounds simple, but most people forget this principle when planning their lives. Professional victims complain about the results in their lives, but it never occurs to them to change the causes.

## ACTIVITIES PRODUCE RESULTS

Suppose I wanted to bake a cake. Since I've never baked a cake before, here is my activity list:

> *First,* add a scoop of flour.
> *Second,* pour in one bottle of beer to make the cake rise.
> *Third,* open a can of frosting and add to the beer and flour.
> *Fourth,* put mixture in metal cooking pan and place it in the microwave oven.
> *Fifth,* avoid sparks and mini-explosions from the microwave oven.

Now, will my activity produce the desired result, the cake of my dreams? No.

No matter how many times I use this recipe, I'll never get a different result. The only way that I can possibly get the cake of my dreams is by *changing my activity.*

That means taking action and trying something different!

### IF YOU ARE NOT HAPPY WITH YOUR LIFE...

Then take a different action and you'll get a different result. Every action or activity will produce a result. If you don't like the result, simply change the action.

For instance, hit your hand with a hammer.

*Ouch! That really hurts.*

Now, hit your hand with a hammer again.

*Ouch! Ouch! That really hurts.*

Now, hit your hand with a hammer again.

*Ouch! Ouch! Ouch! That really, really hurts.*

Get the picture? First you perform an action or activity (hitting your hand with a hammer). Then comes a predictable result from that activity. (*Ouch! Ouch! Ouch!*)

If you want different results, simply change your activity.

How?

Try hitting your friend's hand with a hammer. Now your friend says, "Ouch, ouch!" See, your hand is feeling better already with this simple change of activity.

Let's apply this principle to a less painful example.

Today you get into your car and commute two hours to work. You arrive at the job, get paid peanuts, and you hate every minute you are there.

Tomorrow you get into your car and commute two hours to work. You arrive at the job, get paid peanuts, and you hate every minute you are there.

*Hmm.* I bet if you get into your car tomorrow and commute two hours to work—you just might arrive at the job, get paid peanuts, and hate every minute you are there.

Same activity—same results.

If you want different results, simply change your activity.

How?

Drive to the golf course, or to a new job interview! If you don't like the results you are getting, simply change your activity.

Makes sense, doesn't it?

Why doesn't *everyone* see this? We don't know. It's amazing how many frustrated, desperate people live their lives hoping for different results while performing the exact same activities, year after year after year.

Need more proof? Try this experiment.

## GO DOWN TO THE PUB
### AND LISTEN TO THE LOCALS COMPLAIN

They'll say, "I can't stand my job. Every day it is the same old thing. And my boss is a jerk! The pay is lousy. The traffic is killing me and I can't get a week off when I want."

And you feel like saying to them, "Uh, maybe if you drove somewhere else every morning, you wouldn't end up at the job you hate with the boss you hate."

Of course, free advice such as this can be hazardous to your health.

It's frustrating when you seem to be the only person in the world who can see this *activity/results* concept clearly. You quickly see a solution to almost every complaint, and the rest of the world doesn't see a thing.

Does this happen in network marketing?

Sure. Did you ever hear this statement? "I just can't find any prospects." Your distributor complains, "I can't be successful because I just can't find any prospects. It's my upline's fault, the company's fault, the product's fault, I live too far away from meetings, I don't know anyone. Nobody likes me. The weather is lousy. And I have to work on weekdays!"

Maybe there are some legitimate complaints buried in there. So what? Complaining won't make any of those problems go away. Repeating all these problems to you won't make the weather better or make the distributor's house magically move closer to the meetings.

Your complaining distributor will just have to wake up one day and tell himself: "If you don't like the results, simply change the activity."

All this cause and effect stuff isn't that complicated. Let's apply some of it to your distributors' problems.

*Problem*: **"I have to work on weekdays!"**
*Activity change:* Get a night job instead. Work weekends. Get a job working from home. Win the lottery. Have your spouse get a higher paying job. Take early retirement. See the difference? Your distributor must take personal responsibility for his actions and be willing to change the activity. When the activity changes, so do the results. Let's look at some more problems.

*Problem:* **"The weather is lousy."**
*Activity change:* Move to a better climate. Buy a raincoat. Stay inside.

*Problem:* **"Nobody likes me."**
*Activity change:* Learn to smile. Take a self-improvement course. Meet new people who don't know you.

*Problem:* **"I don't know anyone."**
*Activity change:* Meet new people. Go to a party. Join a community organisation. Advertise. Get married. Spend more time outside.

*Problem:* **"I can't sponsor anybody."**
*Solution:* Start giving presentations. Stop keeping your business a secret. Invite prospects to business meetings. Learn more about your business. Become more professional. Attend training. Learn to smile. Meet more people. Become more positive.

*What do we notice about all of these problems?* The professional victim distributor is asking us to think for him and solve his problems. This is typical behaviour for professional victims. They feel they are powerless and look for a mother or father figure to take care of them and make things right.

*What do we notice about all of these solutions?* All of the solutions require activity and personal responsibility from the distributor. Our distributor is going to have to do something himself to solve his problems.

This means a critical decision is required from the distributor: "Do I quit at the first sign of any resistance, stay a helpless professional victim, and hope somebody takes care of me? Or, do I finally grow up and take responsibility for my own life, for my own results?"

What will your distributor choose?

Some will make the big step to controlling the outcome of their own lives.

Some will run home to mum and say, "My sponsor was mean to me."

Unsuccessful distributors are always looking for someone else to make them successful. They believe that success comes

from outside influences such as the company or their sponsor. Outside influences can't make anyone successful or
unsuccessful.

I've seen this from both sides of the table. Before becoming a full time distributor and letting someone else have all the
worries about running a networking company, I was the man
at the home office pulling my hair out! A couple of times I even
thought of going back into surveying for the British Army!

Without fail, in any given day or week, I'd be on the phone
with my top distributors hearing them tell me how things were
moving quickly, and how business was 'great!' I'd hear about
how the service was fine, the products were unique and wonderful and how this distributor was well on the way to
purchasing their new dream home, luxury car, or obtaining
one of their other goals.

Within hours, sometimes minutes, I'd hear from another
distributor at the opposite end of the success scale. Our
company's products were lousy or average at best; our service
was lousy; and "nobody would buy!" Furthermore, unless I
made the compensation plan more generous right away, they
were going to the competition!

While there are a few "bad apple" companies who are looking out for number one, for the most part companies are run
by people who are trying to succeed just like you are. If the
product is good and the organisation is basically sound, then
there will be people making a fantastic life for themselves in
that opportunity and telling people about the "wonderful opportunity" as if the company had made all these good things
happen. And just as certainly there will be people going further and further into the hole financially and psychologically,
blaming the company for their every misfortune.

Whenever this situation happens, the difference is in the determination of the distributors, not the company. Which distributor will you be?

The real, ugly, disgusting secret in network marketing is that success comes from within the distributor. It's a personal thing.

---

### Author's note:

Just keep dealing with the ones who want your help. That's the best time-saving tip you'll ever hear in your entire networking career!

---

# Attitude + Skill + Effort = Success

One's attitude, skill and effort determines success. If success eludes a distributor, all the distributor has to do is to improve his attitude, skill or effort. Blaming the company, sponsor, or position of the planets won't create success.

Success comes from sponsoring people.

There are several areas that you can choose from to increase your sponsoring effectiveness.

## 1) LEARN MORE ABOUT THE COMPANY'S PRODUCTS.

Why? Because if you become a product expert, prospects will be attracted to your knowledge.

Let's say you sell organic cleaning products. You could learn:

- *How they save your environment.*
- *How they can save money for your customers.*
- *How they can attack specific, hard-to-clean stains.*
- *How they might even help your family stay healthier.*

Now, when a co-worker has a difficult stain on his driveway, who does he turn to for advice? You. You're the expert. You've invested your time to become a source of knowledge that attracts people to you.

## 2) LEARN HOW TO PRESENT YOUR BUSINESS OPPORTUNITY MORE EFFECTIVELY.

When you make your business opportunity presentation clearer, with more benefits, more prospects will join. To achieve this goal you could:

- *Attend more trainings.*
- *Attend a public speaking course.*
- *Read a book on selling.*
- *Practice your presentation on your neighbour.*
- *Learn how to speak in word pictures.*

Now when you give a business opportunity presentation, more prospects will join. You've become more professional, more effective in explaining your business.

## 3) DEVELOP NEW OBSERVATION SKILLS.

There are literally thousands of prospects in your natural, local market, but you must learn to recognise them. When distributors complain about no available prospects, they don't mean there are no prospects in their area or natural market. What they are saying is: "I can't see any prospects that I can talk to."

Professional network marketers have more prospects than they can possibly contact or service. Why? They've developed the skill of recognising prospects where amateur networkers see none.

How are you going to develop that skill?

- *Take the prospecting course from your networking company.*
- *Take your professional sponsor to lunch and learn their secrets of observation.*
- *Learn new listening skills.*
- *Learn more about people's needs and wants.*
- *Notice what people say, and why they are saying it.*

Now, when you leave your front door in the morning, you're literally assaulted with dozens of potential prospect possibilities. I've just mentioned three areas that could help you sponsor more people. It's up to you to pick one of these areas, or to choose a different skill that will help you sponsor more people.

In each area, there are several suggestions on how to achieve proficiency in that skill. Don't try all of the suggestions right away. Simply pick one suggestion and start small.

Remember that big achievements are a result of small sized achievable goals.

---

### Just another reminder:

Did you notice that all three suggestions to help you sponsor more people refer to something you must do? None of the suggestions deal with changing other people. Success and happiness are truly within you, not within other people.

# Prospect or Suspect?

Prepare yourself for some amazing conversations. Now that we see how activities produce results, and how changing activities can change results, most problems seem easy to solve.

Unfortunately, the prospects you talk to won't see or understand these principles. This is what will make your future conversations very, *very* weird. Here is a typical conversation with a prospect who wants to change his future:

**Prospect:** Okay, I want financial independence. I want enough money to take nice holidays with my family or to have enough money for the best medical care if they need it. I love my family, but I also want to do something for me. I don't want to work my whole life helping my boss accumulate enough money for his next mansion. I think there is more in life; more to *my* life. Maybe I could visit Australia for six months. Or, maybe I could go back to school and learn a new language, or learn to paint.

**You:** So, what are you going to *do* about it.

**Prospect:** I don't know.

**You:** Tomorrow, are you going to go wake up, drive to work, and come home again at 6:30 p.m.?

**Prospect:** Yes.

**You:** Are you going to do that again the following day? The following month?

**Prospect:** I guess so.

**You:** For fifteen years you've been going to your job and returning at 6:30 p.m. Where has it got you so far?

**Prospect:** I earn enough to pay the mortgage, buy food and clothes, make payments on my car, and enough to make minimum payments on my credit cards.

**You:** And after fifteen years of earning money, how much of the money is left for you?

**Prospect:** I have less than £3,000 in the bank.

**You:** If you live the next fifteen years the same way as the past fifteen years, how much will you have in the bank?

**Prospect:** Maybe £6,000, if I'm lucky.

**You:** So if you keep doing the same activity, would you agree you'll get the same results?

**Prospect:** I guess so.

**You:** So what are you going to *do* about it? Are you going to change the activity so that you get a different result?

**Prospect:** I don't think so. I can't quit my job. And, the hour or two I have to eat dinner, relax and watch television before I retire is the only time I have to myself. I can't change what I'm doing now. Maybe I should just hope that all of a sudden I get a different result....

**You:** No. If you don't change activities, please don't expect your results to change.

**Prospect:** Sorry, I really can't change what I'm doing. What else do you suggest?

*Whoops!* No personal responsibility here. Now the person is making it your responsibility to come up with a solution for his problem. He won't even accept the responsibility to work on his own problem.

# Even a Blind Squirrel Can Find Acorns If He Gets Under An Oak Tree In The Autumn!

You don't have to be a perfectionist to reach your goals. Sure there are some people who make lists that include "put socks on" every morning and reach their goals, but you don't have to become one of them to set goals and reach them.

Squirrels don't have to be experts in math, economics, goal setting, and motivation to store up enough acorns for winter. They just have to be sitting under the tree when the nuts fall and then pick them up!

Even blind, deaf squirrels whose sense of smell is so bad they confuse skunk odour with *eau de cologne* can get the acorns they need—if they're sitting under the tree at the right time.

So why don't most network marketers or other small business people reach their goal? Because they aren't "sitting under the tree."

Let's take a test. What would happen to squirrels if they were like most networkers?

A. They would have plenty of acorns
B. They would attend weekly meetings conducted by squirrels with plenty of acorns
C. Most would starve.
D. Answers B and C.

*Correct!* D was the right answer. Most would starve, but at least they'd go to meetings!

Think about it. If squirrels behaved like most networkers, they would write big lists about what to do, but never do anything. Here's what the list might look like:

1) *Find tree.*
2) *Analyse species of tree.*
3) *Compare relative productivity of several trees.*
4) *Make up more lists about trees.*

And when they had finished making lists, the squirrels would think about rolling in thousands of acorns and having an organisation to pick acorns for them. These squirrels talk about trees all the time. They think about trees. They attend meetings about trees. And they believe in trees. But they never sit out under trees.

Then there would be squirrels that weren't sure what to do once they got out under the tree. The acorns are all around them but they'd run from place to place under the tree asking, "Is this the right acorn?"

Can this acorn use the Internet?

Will this acorn be able to invest £1,000?

Does this acorn have network marketing experience?

Has this acorn been spoiled by network marketing already?

Is this acorn professional enough to join my acorn pile?

Will this acorn attend acorn meetings?

Sometimes during this entire running around, they even remember to pick up an acorn or two along the way, but these are some very tired and hungry squirrels.

Some squirrels even make it 'big' in the acorn business. They have a palatial tree with a large spacious hole for their acorns. They would even write books for other squirrels to read about getting acorns. There's no harm in telling all the secrets of the acorn business because most squirrels just dream about acorns instead of *going out and getting them*.

Other squirrels believe that the acorn business is a rip-off.

They write to the head squirrel complaining about the acorn business. The head squirrel gets his acorns from the taxes the other squirrels pay, so he's forgotten how hard it is to pick acorns and tends to believe what these other squirrels say about what a rip-off the acorn business is. He wants to regulate the acorn business, so that only large, well-established squirrels can work in that industry and then hire all the other incompetent squirrels who can't work on their own.

But a few very smart squirrels just sit out under the acorn trees, and when the acorns fall, they gather them up and store them for winter. Some make acorn achievement lists. Some don't. Some share their successful acorn gathering techniques with other squirrels. Some don't. Some work with a particular species of acorn. Some work with all the acorns. But the successful squirrels have one thing in common. They know where to position themselves and know what to do when an acorn comes along.

### If network marketers were like squirrels,

1. We'd have our overall goal in sight at all times. We'd know where the acorns were and how many we'd have to find, to stock up for the winter.

2. We'd also know how to pick acorns and store them for winter.

3. Then we'd go to work. Sometimes we'd have great, intricate lists of what to do. Sometimes we'd have simple lists. Either way, we'd go where there are acorns. We'd be on the lookout for people to talk

to. We'd remember to start conversations and hand out tapes. We'd stop worrying about all the other non-essentials and do the basic things that help us reach our overall goal.

Squirrels don't need too much education to do what they do. Yet they can be successful by just sitting out under oak trees and picking up the acorns.

You can be successful in network marketing by just going where the prospects are *and talking to them.*

# Precious Stones, Small Pebbles And Shifting Sand

Success is very much about being the best it's possible for you to be. Too many people try to measure success in terms of money and material things and become very focussed in that direction – to the detriment of everything else.

My Mother used to tell me that

"You can't put an old head on young shoulders"!

I think she was trying to tell me that as you get older you start to see life differently. For most of us, we realise too late in life, what really is important. Don't just have materialistic goals. We all need to stop and "smell the roses" on our journey through life

So find the space and time for all the things that you hold dear – your family, friends and dreams. Lower priorities can take up the remaining space as highlighted by this next story.

A wise old professor took a large beaker half-filled with water and put in some large precious stones till the water came almost to the brim. He asked the class:

"Can the beaker take anymore stones?"

*No*, said the students.

The professor produced a bucket containing small pebbles and put them into the beaker. The water level went up to the brim.

"Do you think there is room for anything else in the beaker?"

*No*, said the students again.

The professor produced a bag of fine sand and slowly poured it into the beaker. The sand slithered into the crevices between the glittering stones and small pebbles. The water remained at the brim.

"What's the lesson here?" he asked.

One student said: "That no matter how full your schedule is, you can always cram more in."

"Wrong," said the professor. "I want you to understand that the contents of this beaker should represent your life.

The precious stones are the important things - your family, your health, your friends - things that if everything else was lost and only they remained, your life would still be full.

The pebbles are the other things that matter like your job, your house, your car. The sand is everything else. The small stuff." "If you put the sand into the jar first, there is no room for the pebbles or the stones. The same goes for your life. If you spend all your time and energy on the small stuff, you will never have room for the things that are important to you.

Pay attention to the things that are critical to your happiness. Play with your children. Look after your health. Take your partner out to dinner. There will always be time to go to work, clean the house, and fix the plumbing." "Take care of the precious stones first - the things that really matter. Set your priorities. The rest is just sand."

*"The lesson is that you must put the precious stones in first – the things that are important to you, your family, friendships, dreams and goals. After that, you can put in the pebbles and fill the crevices with sand – the things that aren't so important".*

# The ABCD Of Life

Someone once said to me, "Life is iffy." He went on to explain that when you looked at the word life the middle two letters spelt 'if.' Life is indeed 'Iffy.' In fact, life can be downright unfair sometimes. But generally speaking, the more you put in, the more you get out. And the less you put in, the less you can take out.

I would like to give you an edge, something that I discovered several years ago: a simple formula for success that I call the ABCD of life: *Attitude*, *Belief*, *Commitment* and *Desire*.

## ATTITUDE

On my journey from failure to success, I met a remarkable man who I shall call Paul. We became friends, but more importantly he also became my mentor. Paul was everything I wanted to be. He was successful, always positive, a tremendous public speaker and admired and respected by everyone who met him. One day I asked him the question, "How do you maintain a positive attitude about situations, even when they appear to be pretty negative?"

He replied, "Each morning I wake up and say to myself, 'Paul, you have two choices today. You can choose to be in a good mood, or you can choose to be in a bad mood.' I choose to be in a good mood. Each time something bad happens, I can choose to be a victim, or I can choose to learn from it. I choose to learn from it. Every time someone comes to me complaining, I can choose to accept their complaining, or I can point out the positive side of life. I choose the positive side of life."

"It can't be that easy," I protested.

"Yes, it is," Paul said. "Life is all about choices. When you cut away all the junk, every situation is a choice. You choose how you react to situations. You choose how people will affect your mood. You choose to be in a good or bad mood. The bottom line is, it's *your choice* how you live life."

Several years ago a large group of natives were discovered living on a remote island. Within weeks of the discovery, a couple of shoe salesmen were sent by their respective companies to the island. When the first salesman arrived he wandered around for an hour and then called his company on a mobile phone. "Don't bother," he said. "No one here wears shoes."

When the second salesman arrived a day later, he also wandered around for an hour before excitedly calling his company. "You're not going to believe this—no one wears shoes here yet! You had better send a full container just for starters!"

Same situation—just a different attitude!

## BELIEF

As we journey through life, we undertake a wide range of commitments with varying levels of belief. In network marketing, I often tell distributors that, "Real success comes not when you get into your business, but when the business gets into you." When you really believe in your opportunity, people will recognise your deep-rooted belief and join your organisation.

Several years ago in South Africa there was a drought. It hadn't rained for months and the farmers were becoming increasingly worried that their crops would fail. Finally, they got together to talk through this grave situation. After much discussion, one farmer got up and suggested they all went to church on Sunday to pray for rain. That Sunday, all the churches for hundreds of miles were packed with farmers and their families, and there was much praying for rain.

On the way home, a little girl who had gone with her family to church looked up at her father and said, "I know why we went to church today, it was to pray for rain, but do you believe—I mean *really* believe—it's going to rain now?" The father looked down lovingly at his young daughter and said, "Of course I do." In response to this, the daughter looked puzzled for a few moments and then exclaimed, "Then why didn't you or any of the other farmers bring umbrellas to church?"

## COMMITMENT

We tend to make commitments when we are assured of certain results. For example, we make a commitment to go to work every day because we expect to get paid at the end of the month.

Many of us have had the pleasure of bring up children. Do you remember when they were about eleven months old and just about to take their first fumbling, stumbling steps. You get all excited and tell the family to come over on Sunday to watch John walk. Sure enough, everyone turns up with cameras in hand to catch this unique moment in time. Eventually, when everyone is ready, Dad holds John and says, "OK, Son, walk to Mummy." Dad gives him a little encouraging push and John's on his way across the room towards Mum's outstretched arms. Halfway there, John stumbles and falls over. Now let me tell you what *doesn't* happen. Dad doesn't walk over to John, pick him up by the nappy and throw him back into his play pen saying, " That's it, Kid. You just blew it!" Of course not. Dad picks him up, dusts him down and sends him on his way again. The parents know that even if John doesn't achieve his walk today, he will in a few days' time. They make a commitment to keep encouraging their child until he succeeds.

## HALF-HEARTED COMMITMENTS WILL ALWAYS PRODUCE HALFHEARTED RESULTS

When I talk about commitment at network marketing meetings, I often challenge everyone to introduce ten new people into their business within the next seven days. A few people respond positively until I add that any one who successfully achieves this will receive a special bonus of £10,000! Suddenly, everyone is on the edge of their seats, leaning forward. You can visibly see the level of commitment going through the roof. They suddenly see the reward up front and guaranteed. Nothing is going to stop them recruiting those ten new distributors. So what changed? Well let's look first at what didn't change:

1. The Company
2. The Product range
3. The general public
4. Their sponsor
5. Their upline
6. Their downline
7. Their spouse

What *did* change was their commitment to their business. When you are totally committed, nothing will stop you succeeding. (I also try to remember to tell them that I was joking about the £10,000 bonus!)

## DESIRE

I'm a great believer in taking time out of our busy lives to meditate. I just sit quietly and think. It's hard to watch a glorious sunset and not be filled with a feeling of wonder. To sit in your garden and quietly marvel at Mother Nature at work. It always awakens in me an urge to do more with my life. A desire to achieve and develop new skills. We all have the potential to do far more than we believe possible.

## PRESIDENT KENNEDY

In 1960, President John F. Kennedy said that within the next ten years America would put a man on the moon! He brought the very best scientists and engineers together and told them to go to work on the project. Six months later, at their first progress meeting, the President was informed that it was an impossible task and that at least eight million new parts had to be invented, designed and made. Undeterred, the President told them to continue. A year later, at the second progress meeting, the President was again confronted by the engineers and scientists. "It is impossible," they told him. Again they were ordered to continue. Well, to cut a long story short, in 1969 Neil Armstrong took that first great step for mankind on the surface of the moon.

What a great man of dreams and desires! President Kennedy certainly believed in the saying, "Whatever the mind of man can conceive and believe in—he can achieve it."

# And Finally...

If you really want to change your life, the first thing you must now do is to change your current actions. Otherwise the old saying becomes a reality:
"If you always do what you've always done, you'll always get what you always got!"
But if we change our actions, we will get different results!

Here's a great story to inspire you

## THE DAFFODIL PRINCIPAL

Several times my daughter had telephoned to say,
"Mother, you must come see the daffodils before they are over."
I wanted to go, but it was a two-hour drive from Laguna to Lake Arrowhead.
"I will come next Tuesday," I promised, a little reluctantly, on her third call. Next Tuesday dawned cold and rainy. Still, I had promised, and so I drove there. When I finally walked into Carolyn's house and hugged and greeted my grandchildren, I said,
"Forget the daffodils, Carolyn! The road is invisible in the clouds and fog, and there is nothing in the world except you and these children that I want to see bad enough to drive another inch!"
My daughter smiled calmly and said,
"We drive in this all the time, Mother."
"Well, you won't get me back on the road until it clears, and then I'm heading for home!" I assured her.
"I was hoping you'd take me over to the garage to pick up my car."
"How far will we have to drive?"
"Just a few blocks," Carolyn said. "I'll drive. I'm used to this."
After several minutes, I had to ask, "Where are we going? This isn't the way to the garage!"

"We're going to my garage the long way," Carolyn smiled, "by way of the daffodils."

"Carolyn," I said sternly, "please turn around."

"It's all right, Mother, I promise. You will never forgive yourself if you miss this experience."

After about twenty minutes, we turned onto a small gravel road and I saw a small church. On the far side of the church, I saw a hand-lettered sign that read, "Daffodil Garden." We got out of the car and each took a child's hand, and I followed Carolyn down the path. Then, we turned a corner of the path, and I looked up and gasped. Before me lay the most glorious sight. It looked as though someone had taken a great vat of gold and poured it down over the mountain peak and slopes.

The flowers were planted in majestic, swirling patterns-great ribbons and swaths of deep orange, white, lemon yellow, salmon pink, saffron, and butter yellow. Each different-coloured variety was planted as a group so that it swirled and flowed like its own river with its own unique hue. There were five acres of flowers.

"But who has done this?" I asked Carolyn.

"It's just one woman," Carolyn answered. "She lives on the property. That's her home."

Carolyn pointed to a well kept A frame house that looked small and modest in the midst of all that glory. We walked up to the house. On the patio, we saw a poster.

"Answers to the Questions I Know You Are Asking" was the headline.

The first answer was a simple one.

"50,000 bulbs," it read.
The second answer was,
"One at a time, by one woman. Two hands,
two feet, and very little brain."
The third answer was,
"Began in 1958."

There it was, The Daffodil Principle.
For me, that moment was a life-changing experience.

I thought of this woman whom I had never met, who, more than
forty years before, had begun-one bulb at a time-to bring her
vision of beauty and joy to an obscure mountain top. Still, just
planting one bulb at a time, year after year, had changed the world.
This unknown woman had forever changed the world in which
she lived. She had created something of indescribable
magnificence, beauty, and inspiration.

"It makes me sad in a way," I admitted to Carolyn. "What might I
have accomplished if I had thought of a wonderful goal thirty-five
or forty years ago and had worked away at it 'one bulb at a time'
through all those years. Just think what I might have been able to
achieve!"

My daughter summed up the message of the day in her usual direct
way. "Start tomorrow," she said.

We convince ourselves that life will be better after we get
married, and start a family. Then we are frustrated that our children
aren't old enough and we'll be more content when they are.
After that, we're frustrated that we have teenagers to deal with. We
will certainly be happy when they are out of that stage. We tell

ourselves that our life will be complete when our spouse gets his or her act together, when we get a better car, when we are able to travel to exotic locations, or when we retire. The truth is there's no better time to be happy than right now. If not now, when? Your life will always be filled with challenges. It's best to admit this to yourself and decide to be happy anyway.

So, treasure every moment that you have and treasure it more because you shared it with someone special, special enough to spend your time with... and remember that time waits for no one.

So, stop waiting...
Until your car or home is paid off
Until you get a new car or home
Until your kids leave the house
Until you go back to school
Until you finish school
Until you lose weight.
Until you gain weight
Until you get married
Until you get a divorce
Until you have children
Until you retire
Until summer
Until spring
Until winter
Until Autumn
Until you die

*There is no better time than right now to be happy.*
*Happiness is a journey, not a destination. Enjoy it!*

# What I've Learned

I've learned...
   that it's taking me a long time to become the
   person I want to be.

I've learned...
   that maturity has more to do with what types of
   experiences you've had and what you've learned
   from them and less to do with how many birthdays
   you've celebrated.

I've learned...
   that no matter how good a friend is, they're going
   to hurt you every once in a while and you must
   forgive them for that.

I've learned...
   that you should never tell a child their dreams are
   unlikely or outlandish. Few things are more
   humiliating, and what a tragedy it would be if they
   believed it.

I've learned...
   that no matter how bad your heart is broken the
   world doesn't stop for your grief.

I've learned...
   that our background and circumstances may have
   influenced who we are, but we are responsible for
   who we become.

I've learned...

that just because two people argue, it doesn't
mean they don't love each other; and just because
they don't argue, it doesn't mean they do.

I've learned...

that we don't have to change friends if we understand that friends change.

I've learned...

that you shouldn't be so eager to find out a secret.
It could change your life forever.

I've learned...

that no matter how you try to protect your children, they will eventually get hurt and you will hurt
in the process.

I've learned...

that people who don't even know you, can change
your life in a matter of hours.

I've learned...

that even when you think you have no more to
give, when a friend cries out to you, you will find
the strength to help.

I've learned...

that credentials on the wall do not make you a
decent human being.

I've learned...
> that it isn't always enough to be forgiven by
> others. Sometimes you have to learn to forgive
> yourself.

I've learned...
> that the people you care about most in life are
> taken from you too soon.

I've learned...
> that it's hard to determine where to draw the line
> between being nice and not hurting people's
> feelings, and standing up for what you believe.

I've learned...
> that you cannot make someone love you. All you
> can do is be someone who can be loved. The rest
> is up to them.

I've learned...
> that no matter how much I care, some people just
> don't care back.

I've learned...
> that it takes years to build up trust, and only
> seconds to destroy it.

I've learned...
> that it's not what you have in your life but who you
> have in your life that counts.

I've learned...

    that you can get by on charm for about fifteen
    minutes. After that, you'd better know something.

I've learned...

    that you shouldn't compare yourself to the best
    achievements of others.

I've learned...

    that you can do something in an instant that will
    give you heartache for life.

I've learned...

    that you should always leave loved ones with
    loving words. It may be the last time you see them.

I've learned...

    that you can keep going long after you can't.

I've learned...

    that we are responsible for what we do, no matter
    how we feel.

I've learned...

    that either you control your attitude or it controls
    you.

I've learned...

    that regardless of how hot and steamy a relation-
    ship is at first, the passion fades and there had
    better be something else to take its place.

I've learned...
> that heroes are the people who do what has to be
> done when it needs to be done, regardless of the
> consequences.

I've learned...
> that money is a lousy way of keeping score.

I've learned...
> that my best friend and I can do anything or
> nothing and have the best time.

I've learned...
> that sometimes the people you expect to kick you
> when you're down will be the ones to help you get
> back up.

I've learned...
> that sometimes when I'm angry 1 have the right to
> be angry, but that doesn't give me the right to be
> cruel.

I've learned...
> that true friendship continues to grow, even over
> the longest distance. The same goes for true love.

I've learned...
> that just because someone doesn't love you the
> way you want them to, doesn't mean they don't
> love you with all they have.

I've learned...
> that two people can look at the exact same thing
> and see something totally different.

## Just For Today

Just for today, I will live through the next twelve hours and not tackle my whole life's problems at once.

Just for today, I will improve my mind. I will learn something useful. I will read something that requires effort, thought, and concentration.

Just for today, I will be agreeable. I will look my best, speak in a well modulated voice, be courteous and considerate.

Just for today, I will not find fault with a friend, relative or colleague. I will not try to change or improve anybody but myself.

Just for today, I will have a program. I might not follow it exactly, but I will have it. I will save myself from two enemies: hurry and indecision.

Just for today, I will exercise my character in three ways. I will do a good turn and keep it a secret. If anyone finds out it will not count.

Just for today, I will do two things I don't want to do, just for exercise.

Just for today, I will be unafraid to enjoy what is beautiful and believe that as I give to the world, the world will give back to me.

## AN INVITATION FROM THE AUTHOR

I sincerely hope you enjoyed this book and that it will inspire you to take action. I trust you find my thoughts and ideas useful. I would really welcome your experiences as a result of reading this book. You can contact me personally on:

Tel: 00 44 (1) 635 866895
Fax: 00 44 (1) 635 873268
Email: C21Church@AOL.com

I look forward to hearing from you.

John Church

## TRAINING AND SEMINARS

If you would like to know more about John's keynote presentations, please contact Network Marketing Support at the following address:

Heathcote House
1 Heathcote Road
Bordon
Hants GU35 0BN

Tel: 00 44 (0) 1420 473383
Fax: 00 44 (0) 1420 476140
Email: orders@aireau.co.uk
Website: www.aireau.co.uk

# The Magic of Goal Setting
### *is priced at £8.95*

*For the professional leader who wishes to take advantage of the author's generous quantity discounts, the following schedule applies:-*

| | |
|---|---|
| *1 - 9* | *£8.95* |
| *10 +* | *£8.00* |
| *25+* | *£7.00* |
| *50+* | *£6.00* |
| *100+* | *£5.50* |
| *500+* | *£4.50* |

*Please note that individual print runs are available for 'Book of the Month', Special Trainings or Distributor Packs.*

*Please contact* Network Marketing Support *to discuss your Individual requirements - the book cover can also be adapted to reflect individual Corporate identities.*

To order – contact:-

**Network Marketing Support**
**Heathcote House**
**1 Heathcote Road**
**Bordon**
**Hants GU35 0BN**
**Tel:  01420 473383**

Fax: 01420 476140
Email: orders@aireau.co.uk
Website: www.aireau.co.uk

*(Network Marketing Support is a trade name of AirEau Fittings Limited)*

## Goals

Written goals like shopping list.

If items are written down on a list you will remember them. If not written down. - although you know you want them, they will not jump out at you from the shelves in the shop. - Written down, they seem to present themselves. = Reticular Activity.